D1260596

Hudson Valley

History & Mystery

Michael Adamovic

SCHIFFER PUBLISHING

4880 Lower Valley Road • Atglen, PA 19310

Other Schiffer Books by the Author:

Hudson Valley Reflections: Illustrated Travel and Field Guide
ISBN: 978-0-7643-5346-8

Other Schiffer Books on Related Subjects:

Hudson Valley Haunts: Historic Driving Tours
Linda Zimmermann
ISBN: 978-0-7643-3173-2

Spooky Hudson Valley
Marianna Boncek
ISBN: 978-0-7643-3384-2

Library of Congress Control Number: 2020930735

Designed by Jack Chappell
Cover design by Jack Chappell

Type set in Foxlite/Adelon Antique/Adobe Garamond

ISBN: 978-0-7643-6024-4
Printed in India

Published by Schiffer Publishing, Ltd.
4880 Lower Valley Road
Atglen, PA 19310
Phone: (610) 593-1777; Fax: (610) 593-2002
E-mail: Info@schifferbooks.com
Web: www.schifferbooks.com

Dedication

For Meagan—my inspiration and love.

All photos by Michael Adamovic

Contents

Introduction

Over the span of only four centuries, southern New York has been under the leadership of several nations, all of which have left their individual mark on the region. First came the Native Americans, then the Dutch and English, and finally, after the War for Independence, us—the Americans. The struggle to maintain power or wrest it from others requires significant momentum and pulls a great many people into the fray, each harboring their own strong hopes and opinions. Embroiled in conflict, the region, like a vast foaming, bubbling cauldron, spits out heroes and villains, legends and lore.

From every untimely death can rise a ghost. Behind the veil of a shadowy, uncertain past, grand tales of fancy take flight that may or may not contain a hint of truth. What's more, each group imbued with their own unique beliefs scratched their heads when pondering those of others. The great heterogeneity of cultures in the Hudson Valley and Catskills is precisely why today southern New York is endowed with a greater quantity of mysteries, superstitions, and shadowy tales than neighboring areas and states.

Many prominent landmarks throughout the region are especially suffused with Native American lore. This is unsurprising given that they had the longest duration of occupancy and when the Europeans arrived it was a literal clash between worlds—the Old and the New. European notions and values were on a completely different plane than that of the region's aboriginal inhabitants. Puzzled, even stunned, by various activities that they couldn't quite grasp, Europeans twisted them into things they could.

For instance, in the early 1600s, when the Dutch sailed past an expansive flat rock that jutted into the Hudson just north of Newburgh, they frequently encountered large gatherings of natives there frantically dancing, jumping, and singing around enormous bonfires. To the natives, this was a religious exercise meant to ask favor of the Great Spirit. But to devout Christians who worshiped quietly and with restraint, these energetic activities, quite frankly, terrified them. In their minds, worship of this nature—polar opposite of what the Dutch engaged in—must be directed toward God's opposite. So, the Dutch named this place the Duyvil's Danskammer, or Devil's Dance Chamber.

This spot was one of the most well-documented sacred sites of Native Americans, certainly in New York, and perhaps in the entire Northeast. These ceremonies continued for another 50 years after the Dutch first witnessed them until the Indians were gradually pushed out of the area. Legend has it that during religious ceremonies aimed at eliciting favor for an upcoming hunt or war, if a harmless animal appeared, success was foretold, but if a predator showed, it was regarded as an ill omen.

From historical accounts, the Danskammer was a flat-topped half-acre rock that was separated from the mainland by a marshy area and covered with beautiful white cedars. It sat at the edge of a peninsula opposite the Wappingers Creek. Today, a power plant occupies this once-sacred site, not a trace of its former beauty remaining.

Another interesting landmark known as the Turk's Face has also disappeared. Sitting toward the base of Breakneck Ridge, a rocky promontory similar in nature to New Hampshire's renowned Old Man of the Mountain once protruded from a steep cliff. So striking was the resemblance to a human countenance that some observers noted that the promontory actually surpassed the symmetry of some human faces! It was well regarded, and steamships would often ferry people out to it so they could marvel at the natural masterpiece. But in 1846, it was obliterated in an instant when an uncaring quarry owner blasted it with dynamite, all for the sake of "progress."

Despite the richness of mysterious and historic sites that still exist across the region, it's disheartening to contemplate the willful destruction of even one. As the old saying goes, "They don't make them like they used to." In today's age, where nearly everything is documented and cameras are ubiquitous, a good mystery is hard to find. The Indians are gone. The age of exploration has all but ended. We have a seemingly long and flat, languid course ahead of us. Generally speaking, new sites of this nature aren't arising. We must protect and cherish what remains. The petroglyphs, stone chambers, historic sites, and even waterfalls in this book are a tangible link to the past. It's one thing to read about them, but another to actually have a chance to visit and walk in the footsteps of those who came before us.

It's my hope that the reader will take advantage of the directions listed in this book. By getting out there, you'll have a chance to formulate your own theories and opinions regarding the origin of sites such as the stone chambers and Balanced Rock, or perhaps even figure out where the cutthroat gangster Dutch Schultz hid his loot.

Many of these sites have an aspect of the supernatural about them. Whether or not you believe in such things, I ask you to surrender for a moment. Appreciate the richness of tales, the fertility of the land, and the varied imaginations that have breathed life into the inanimate.

The Capture of Major John André

On the east side of Broadway in the center of Tarrytown lies Patriots Park, a small green space landlocked by schools, private residences, and shops. At first glance, it appears to be a rather mundane open space in an otherwise congested city, mostly used by dog walkers, tired tourists who need a few minutes to convalesce, and generally those who have a propensity to "tarry." But inspection of an aging, neglected monument and historical marker near the sidewalk running along the busy thoroughfare shows that this seemingly ordinary place was where one of the American Revolution's—indeed one of the nation's—greatest treasonous plots was foiled, not by some shining, decorated hero, but rather collectively by a trio of militiamen, who have often been labeled as thieves and marauders.

It is here that the unfortunate Major John André of the British Army, carrying papers given to him by the treacherous Benedict Arnold for the takeover of West Point, was captured on September 23, 1780.

The story begins two days earlier on the other side of the Hudson, at a dock just south of Haverstraw that sat at the base of the looming Long Clove Mountain. At this location, a secret midnight rendezvous was arranged so Benedict Arnold could pass on information to the enemy vital to the storming and capture of the fortress at West Point. The Hudson Highlands were of the utmost importance to both sides, since the area linked New England to the rest of the country. If the British could take control of the region, they would effectively sever communication, the transport of supplies, and the movement of troops between New England and the southern states, hastening the downfall of the American cause.

André, ferried across Haverstraw Bay from the *Vulture*, a British warship moored off Croton Point, met Arnold at the dock, and in perfect darkness the two discussed everything from troop numbers at West Point to Arnold's compensation for his defection from the Continental Army. Shortly before dawn, the first of a series of misfortunes began for André. The men who had transported him to his meeting with

Arnold refused to row him back to the *Vulture*, citing concerns that the tide was against them. They would not be able to return before daylight and therefore would likely be spotted crossing the Hudson. Because the two still had much to discuss, André ventured with Arnold back to a nearby house to conclude their discussion, where he would await transport back to his ship the following evening. But shortly after their arrival to the residence, American forces on Croton Point proceeded to bombard the *Vulture* with cannon fire. In order to escape destruction, the ship was forced to flee downstream, leaving André stranded in enemy territory.

Forced to venture back on foot to the British lines in lower Westchester, André removed his uniform and donned a disguise, posing as a merchant by the name of John Anderson. Before André left, Arnold convinced him to carry back a set of documents that listed the fortress's weaknesses. André placed the papers in his stockings. His superior, Sir Henry Clinton, had explicitly warned against both measures, in fear he could be mistaken for a spy. But what was to be done? André was now stranded and seemingly only had this one option to return safely.

André was taken across the Hudson in a barge to Westchester County, a so-called neutral ground where neither side had full control, but where Loyalist "cowboys" and Patriot "skinners" patrolled the area, often wreaking havoc on local inhabitants. On horse, André undertook the long journey back to his compatriots in Dobbs Ferry. Along the way, he was warned by a local that a group of cowboys were recently spotted roaming a stretch of road he was soon to pass. He decided to continue ahead, rather than seeking an alternate route. After all, the cowboys were sure to be friendly to a British officer and would likely hasten his return to his superiors. This bit of news undoubtedly put André at ease but would soon prove disastrous.

A small stream known as Clark's Kill or André Brook bisects Patriots Park and is the dividing line between Tarrytown and Sleepy Hollow.

The Captors' Monument at the entrance of Patriots Park marks the exact spot where Major John André was captured.

As André crossed Clark's Kill in Tarrytown along the Post Road, which is now known as Broadway (Route 9), a man stepped out of the bushes and pointed a gun at him. This was John Paulding, an American, who had only days earlier escaped from British captivity in New York. Two others, David Williams and Isaac Van Wart, soon joined him. The trio, all militiamen, had been sent here to capture cowboys and other suspicious persons. Seeing Paulding wearing a green and red Hessian jacket, André assumed him to be a friend (Hessians were allied to the British) and uttered, "I hope you belong to our party?" "What party?" Paulding issued back. "The lower"—and with that line André sealed his fate.[1]

The "lower party" meant the British, since they occupied southern Westchester, or the lower portion of the county. It's unclear why Paulding was wearing a Hessian jacket on this day—he had obtained it during his escape and used it as a disguise to get back home. It's possible he was unable to obtain another jacket, since they were in short supply, or perhaps he purposely wore it to deceive unsuspecting travelers such as André.

Now smiling, the men played along and told André that they were Loyalist cowboys, and asked him to dismount his horse. Upon doing so, André was informed that they were in fact Americans. Realizing his possibly deadly error, André immediately backpedaled and, in an awkward display, chuckled that a fellow must do anything to get by, and stated that he was actually an American. To prove this, he produced a pass written by Arnold that ensured safe passage to one John Anderson. While the pass had clearly been written by the general, the group was still suspicious and took André aside to search him.

Finding nothing incriminating as they searched his jacket and outerwear, they then instructed him to remove his boots. To this he seemed indifferent. Unfortunately for André, one of the men noticed that his stockings were sagging rather oddly down by the feet, and told him to remove these as well. Three documents were found hidden under each foot. Paulding carefully scanned the documents and, in short time, declared the unfortunate André a spy!

After finding the incriminating documents, the three militiamen asked André what he would give them to let him go. Along with offering them his gold watch and his horse, André promised to pay them "any sum of money" they desired. Later at a military trial of one of Arnold's unwitting accomplices, Paulding is recorded to have forcefully declined the bribe during the encounter by saying, "No, if you would give us two thousand guineas you should not stir one step."[2]

In a letter previously sent by Arnold a few days before all the mayhem began, he had instructed the British that if they also wished to capture Washington during their siege of West Point, that they should attack on the night of the 23rd, since the commander in chief of the American forces would be there to inspect the state of the fortifications. In a grand twist, on this day André, not Washington, would be the one apprehended.

Now a prisoner, André was taken by his captors to the nearest American outpost. Not exactly sure what to make of the situation, the commander sent a letter to Arnold, explaining that a suspicious person bearing a pass with his signature had recently been taken prisoner.

Upon reading the letter the horrified general knew his plot was soon to be fully exposed. His only option now was to flee to the British. After a quick goodbye to his wife, he hopped on his horse and, ignoring the gradual switchbacks of his mountainous route, rode straight down the precipitous slopes at full speed to the banks of the Hudson. He told his bargemen to row him out to the *Vulture* under a white flag, since he had an urgent letter to deliver to someone aboard the ship. Arnold promised them barrels of rum if they made it there and back quickly. Once Arnold was safely aboard, he had the British take his own men prisoner! Arnold would later be given a substantial monetary reward for his efforts and a commission in the British army as a brigadier general.

Efforts were made by the British for André's release, but General Washington would only do so in exchange for them handing over the traitorous Arnold. The British flatly refused, since they felt it would discourage future American defections. And so, André was brought to trial, where he was convicted of espionage and sentenced to death by hanging. Before his execution, André would befriend most who visited him in prison. Many high-ranking officers in the army thought he had been a victim of circumstance, and felt a deep sympathy toward his plight, among them Alexander Hamilton and Benjamin Tallmadge (Washington's head of intelligence). Moreover, there was something about André's habits and demeanor that enthralled. According to the historian Nathaniel Philbrick, at the time of André's execution, he was "surrounded by a coterie of adoring American officers."[3]

At noon on October 2, 1780, on a hill in Tappan, André placed the hangman's noose around his own neck and asked the audience to see that he died a brave man. "The spot was consecrated by the tears of thousands," one eyewitness recounted.[4]

Selflessness or Selfishness?

For their service in thwarting the British plot to take West Point, the men who had captured André were celebrated as heroes. Washington himself awarded each of the men a silver medallion in a special ceremony. After the war, they would additionally receive a $200 yearly pension and a tract of land from the state of New York in gratitude of their service.

Not everyone was convinced of their heroism, however. Years later, when John Paulding petitioned Congress to adjust his pension for inflation, Benjamin Tallmadge, now a member of Congress, derided Paulding and the others in an eloquent address. He was convinced by statements made to him by André that the men were not selfless heroes, but rather a group of men interested chiefly in personal profit. Had the group been able to obtain a ransom for André from the British without the possibility of being captured themselves, they likely would have released him. But they felt the risk was too great and that the best option for a reward would be to turn him over to their fellow Americans. Tallmadge's 1817 address to Congress was effective, thereby preventing the captors from getting any increase in their pensions.

Statue of John Paulding atop the Captors' Monument.

There is evidence to suggest that David Williams and Isaac Van Wart, prior to André's capture, were little more than lawless highwaymen bent solely on self-interest, having dealings with both Loyalists and Patriots. Both men are recorded as having strung up a man in order to get him to reveal where he hid his money, robbing the poor fellow of $1,300 in gold. Still, several early historians believed that most of the negative press about the men was slanderous, and almost lyrically praised them.

It is without doubt that the men played a vital role in the Revolution by averting what would have proved a major blow to the American cause had West Point fallen. And because of this, in 1880, a monument in their honor was erected at the very spot where they had first stopped André a century earlier. Ironically, a man by the name of John Anderson (André's code name) provided the funds to do so.

A Legend Is Born

André died at the young age of 29. While he accepted his fate with dignity and outwardly put on a brave face, below the surface there must have been a seething anger toward Arnold, whom he blamed for his misfortune. André undoubtedly made several blunders on his trek south, but it was Arnold who brought him back behind enemy lines and convinced him to dress as a civilian and take the documents that would eventually bring about his ruin. Some say because of his inner turmoil and untimely demise, André's spirit couldn't rest and so returned to haunt the place of his capture.

"On still autumn nights," a nineteenth-century writer penned, "belated wayfarers sometimes heard the sound of hoofs. A madly galloping horse seemed to approach, but no horse or horseman was visible to the keenest of eyes." The ghostly sounds were never heard south of where André was taken. Most experiences were adjacent to a muddy piece of land known as Wiley's Swamp, at the stream crossing where he was first stopped. In addition to the ghostly sounds, a "formless gray shadow" was said to sometimes whisk by at a furious pace.[5]

Washington Irving eventually worked these encounters into "The Legend of Sleepy Hollow." He writes that ever since André's capture, the spot has "been considered a haunted stream, and fearful are the feelings of the schoolboy who has to pass it after dark."[6]

In many instances it has been incorrectly stated that a towering tulip tree with "gnarled and fantastic" limbs stood at the exact location where André was captured, and therefore was called "Major André's tree."[7] This tree did exist, but it stood around 200 yards farther south, near the current location of Warner Library. It grew in the center of the road and served as a meeting place for those wishing to enlist in the colonial militia during the spring of 1776. Being a major landmark, it quickly became associated with André's nearby capture. Irving mentions that "mournful cries and wailings" emanated from the site of the tree.[8] "The common people," he adds, "regarded it with a mixture of respect and superstition."[9]

Bizarrely, "Major André's tree" was destroyed by a bolt of lightning on the night of the July 21, 1801, the same day that news of Benedict Arnold's death in England reached Tarrytown. It stood 111 feet high and had a circumference of 29 feet.

Intense development of Tarrytown over the years has all but eradicated the specter. Constant illumination from ubiquitous streetlights seems to act as ghost repellent. Moreover, the once-isolated and gloomy Wiley's Swamp, a "marshy and thickly wooded glen," was razed to create Patriots Park.[10] The wild course of André's Brook is now penned in by stone walls and overtopped by a series of bridges. All overt traces of spookiness have vanished. Still, on rare occasions, there are reports of disembodied voices uttering poetic lines in the park. You see, on the day André was captured, the last section of a long poem he authored was published in the *Rivington's Gazette*. Disheartened by the loss of his accustomed scenery, he chants: "The trees you see them cutting yonder / Are all my near relations. / And I, forlorn, implore thine aid / To free the sacred grove."[11]

Getting There

Patriots Park is located a few hundred feet north of Warner Library (121 North Broadway, Tarrytown, NY 10591). The Captors' Monument (41.081777, -73.858274), the site of Major John André's capture in September 1780, is along the sidewalk at the main entrance of the park.

2

Raven Rock

Some mention was made also of the woman in white, that haunted the dark glen at Raven Rock and was often heard to shriek on winter nights before a storm, having perished there in the snow.[12]

—Washington Irving

One of the first published references of Raven Rock appeared in Washington Irving's 1820 short story, "The Legend of Sleepy Hollow." The description he gives of the place and the primary spirit said to haunt the environs of the monolith is brief (a single sentence). But being such an iconic writer, even a distilled tale such as this has managed to ensure that the landmark, which otherwise may have attained a high degree of obscurity, is still well regarded and known to the larger world.

"Raven Rock," says the prominent Westchester County historian Edgar Bacon, "is a detached portion of the steep, rocky, eastern side of Buttermilk Hill, which a deep fissure has long separated from the mass, and the fragment, becoming independent territory, set up a mythology of its own."[13] The blocky mass stands about 60 feet high and looms over an adjacent old carriage road. When the sun hangs low in the sky and the landmark casts a multitude of shadows in the darkened glen, an eerie, foreboding feeling begins to creep over the passerby, and it becomes easy to see why this area has long been reported to be haunted by a multitude of spooks. What makes Raven Rock even more awe inspiring is the forest that surrounds it—a sparse understory and towering trees that look dwarfed standing before the sheer wall of the precipice. Over the years, these aspects helped imbue the site with "a thousand strange stories and superstitions."[14]

The land the monolith sits upon was once owned by John D. Rockefeller and his heirs but is now public property and part of Rockefeller State Park. The Saw Mill River Parkway is only a short distance away, skirting the base of Buttermilk Hill.

Raven Rock in late October.

Unlike many other impressively large boulders and masses of stone in the area that have received their names from a physical resemblance to an object, Raven Rock isn't so named because it's in the shape of a raven. Rather, it received its title from the large flocks of ravens or crows that once gathered atop its flat summit. A nest or two can still be found there today. These ominous creatures are associated with superstition and undoubtedly once helped bolster the gloomy atmosphere surrounding the site.

The main legend of Raven Rock relates to the woman in white that Irving mentions. Most versions of the story are rather vague. It is said that long ago a woman seeking shelter from a blizzard took refuge at Raven Rock beneath a slight overhang, offering her a modicum of protection from the biting winds and blinding snows. It is supposed that she was gathering firewood in the immediate vicinity and was caught off guard by the brewing storm and, after trudging along in it for awhile, became disoriented and weary. Hoping that the storm would weaken, or she would gain some strength after stopping to rest and would then be able to complete the final push home, she made a detour and settled in at the base of the monolith. But unfortunately, neither did the storm abate nor did she regain any energy. Instead, the bitter cold and swirling snows caused her to become drowsy and lethargic. The snow eventually formed a blanket over her, and in short time, she weakly took her last breath of numbing winter air before expiring.

The woman wasn't discovered until spring, when the thick load of winter snow and ice finally melted. She is reported to be buried in the Old Dutch Burying Ground in Sleepy Hollow, though her name has been forgotten.

Her spirit resides at Raven Rock, and during stormy winter weather, she makes herself known to those passing the lonely site of her demise. Some report hearing melancholy cries issuing from the fissures in the rock. There's wide variation in the reports. At times the cries are loud, frightening shrieks, and at others they are almost indistinguishable from the winds. It appears that the woman suits her theatrics to the temperament of the passersby. She does whatever it takes to keep people from lingering at Raven Rock and meeting her unfortunate fate. In this respect, she is perhaps one of the most caring ghosts of the region. Edgar Bacon believed that no other equals "so kindly and Christian a complexion as this poor spectre."[15] Her figure also occasionally takes shape from the snows and mists that envelop the rock in harsh weather.

Another similar specter reputed to haunt the area is that of a "colonial dame," who, chased by amorous cowboys (Loyalist highwaymen), climbed to the top of Raven Rock and jumped off, rather than being subjected to indignities.[16] Her spirit can be heard sobbing from time to time at the scene of her death.

And a third analogous legend involves that of an Indian girl. Lore dictates that the maiden was pursued by a spurned lover, who determined that if he couldn't possess the lovely girl, no one could, and so hatched a plan to kill her. Details are scarce, but somehow a chase ensued through the woods, and the maiden, in an attempt to escape, climbed the rock. The rebuffed man followed close behind and cornered her at the edge. Holding a flint blade in his hand, his purpose was plain. Not wanting to die at the hands of so ignoble a man, she decided to take her own

Raven Rock towers to around 60 feet.

life and leapt off. It is said that Manitou, the Great Spirit, took pity on her and, before she hit the ground, transformed the unlucky girl into a raven. It is believed she still keeps a watchful eye on the spot, visiting in the guise Manitou bestowed upon her as she bravely plummeted toward her doom.

One report from 1905 indicates that Raven Rock was also home to something more tangible and threatening. "I have heard a story," Minna Irving writes, "of a fabulous lizard that lived under the rock, scaly with age, and big as a half-grown alligator." She further adds, "and it is certainly a favorite haunt of snakes."[17] This may be something you want to keep in mind next time you're keen on exploring the crevices and remains of a cave that cut deeply into the base of the monolith. Who knows what scaly creatures it may still hold?

It's interesting to note that Raven Rock was used as a shelter by Sergeant John Dean, a storied soldier of the American Revolution, during the war. He would frequently make a bed at the bottom of the rock, perhaps in the same location once used by the woman in white. While his father's home was only a short distance away, it is likely he thought it prudent to sleep elsewhere to avoid being captured, since he was a well-known patriot living amid the neutral zone—an area where neither the British nor American forces controlled, but where each side continually undertook forays to harass the other. Despite his best efforts of concealment, he found himself surrounded here one day in late 1780 by British troopers, who, catching him off guard, had guns aimed on him from two directions. There was no way he could hope to fight or flee without serious risk of death, and so thinking of his family, he reluctantly surrendered. He was in captivity for only a short time before gaining his release as part of a prisoner exchange.

John Dean was instrumental when it came to the capture of the British Major John André, a spy who carried plans of West Point given to him by none other than Benedict Arnold, as we touched on earlier. On the day of André's capture, Dean assigned the posts for a group of militiamen. He instructed the now-glorified John Paulding, David Williams, and Isaac Van Wart to watch the road leading through the village of Tarrytown for suspicious persons, while Dean and four others formed a separate group a short distance away. As André descended the road and passed the trio, they leapt from their leafy hiding spot, stopped the British officer, and, after a diligent search, found the damning papers. Had Dean not decided to patrol that day or had he chosen different locations for his men to guard, the fate of the Revolution may have been very different.

Brooding in a remote section of Rockefeller State Park, Raven Rock no longer receives the steady influx of visitors it once did when the old carriage road that passed the monolith was active. Today, it is a curious natural landmark that mainly draws admirers of Washington Irving or those interested in the supernatural. The specters said to haunt Raven Rock must indeed be lonelier than ever, rarely ever getting the opportunity to make themselves known since most people aren't likely to wander past after dark—and we all know ghosts almost never show their faces in broad daylight. Still, those who visit on gloomy days with a storm looming in the not-so-far distance just might hear the wailing of the woman in white doing her duty to keep you from becoming her eternal companion.

Getting There

Raven Rock is located in one of the more remote sections of Rockefeller State Park Preserve. There are multiple ways to get there, so it's probably best to consult a trail map: https://parks.ny.gov/parks/attachments/RockefellerTrailMap.pdf. The shortest route to Raven Rock is 1.8 miles one way.

Park along the shoulder of Bedford Road, half a mile north of the entrance to the Stone Barns Center (630 Bedford Road, Tarrytown, NY 10591). There's only a small stretch of road in which to park (41.110085, -73. 820256). Keep an eye out for the numerous "No Parking" signs.

The best way to access the landmark after parking at this location is to walk south along Bedford Road for a couple of hundred feet. Shortly after crossing a stone bridge, a carriage road passing through a field will appear on the left. Follow the unmarked carriage road uphill (there is little to no signage in this area acknowledging this as parkland). **The entire trail system is poorly marked, so carrying a map is a must.** Once you are at the top of the grassy hill, there are a few different routes that can be taken to reach Raven Rock (41.096505, -73.816471).

3 Bear Rock Petroglyph

Just prior to European colonization, there were up to 12,000 Native Americans living in the Hudson Valley. They called the region home since shortly after the end of the last Ice Age. An excavated rockshelter in the Black Dirt Region of southern Orange County shows a human presence dating back to at least 9500 BCE. Remarkably, even with such a long habitation as this, there is relatively little evidence to show they existed here at all. Rather than ruthlessly subjugating nature like their European cousins, native peoples were careful not to alter the land more than necessary, believing that everything from the largest of animals to lakes, trees, and even stones is imbued with a spirit. While they were not perfect stewards of the land as we have often been taught, they lived more in harmony with nature than against it.

Most of what was left behind—simple artifacts ranging from arrowheads to shattered pottery—is now buried underground and only revealed through careful archeological excavations. One visible testament to their existence in the Hudson Valley to those who have not made archeology a career are the petroglyphs they created.

Compared to sites out West, where, in some cases, carvings litter vast stretches of canyon, petroglyphs in the Northeast are few and far between. While far from the precise, meticulously carved hieroglyphics of Egypt, Native American carvings held a comparable function, crude as some may be. No written language existed, and the petroglyphs couldn't have been read, but they were sometimes employed to record a story or important event. Petroglyphs were able to spark a memory.

They served a similar, though more lasting, purpose with the "memory holes" of southern New England.[18] Wherever a remarkable event took place along an Indian path, a hole about a foot deep would be dug to commemorate it. It was the duty of every Indian to maintain the holes and remember what had transpired at each spot. In this way, history was transmitted orally from generation to generation.

Petroglyph of a reclining black bear.

Apart from serving as a record, petroglyphs were utilized for religious purposes. They were created to commune with spirits, to give thanks, and to seek luck with everything from hunting to fertility. Moreover, some served more-mundane uses, such as territorial markers. Some may even have been simple doodles created from boredom.

Regardless of why they were created, today they stand as interesting pieces of art that help give us better insight to the lives of the various Hudson Valley tribes. Human and animal effigies, in addition to whimsical shapes, are common portrayals. Rarer petroglyphs marked astronomical events or bodies, such as the alignment of the constellations in the heavens.

Found along the shores of the Hudson River to the interior of the Catskills, and even in the now-bustling center of New York City, these petroglyphs are widely scattered. But the scarcity of the carvings, along with the fact that many of them are inaccessible, being on private property or in the middle of nowhere, poses challenges to those wishing to view the ancient rock art. Ward Pound Ridge Reservation in eastern Westchester County offers one of the best opportunities to glimpse one up close. The county-owned park contains a handful, the most prominent and best among them being the Bear Rock petroglyph, conveniently located right alongside a hiking trail.

Bear Rock is a 7-foot-high granite boulder that is a little wider than it is tall. It's a glacial erratic and sits in a forest near the top of a small mountain, approximately 2 miles from the nearest trailhead. The boulder itself is in the general shape of a bear head. But it receives its name from a figure etched into the stone that resembles a reclining black bear. This resemblance is quite striking. Part of the neck and back are

Bear Rock is in the shape of a bear head.

positioned on a curved edge of the boulder, so as to give the animal a 3-D effect.

A total of nineteen separate designs are carved into Bear Rock, many of them being small ellipses. All these petroglyphs are located on the western face. Unfortunately, none are as clear as the figure of the bear. Nicholas Shoumatoff, a park official who discovered Bear Rock in 1971, noted the presence of a "twin deer" head, a turkey or a grouse, and a star.[19] And there is also a serpentlike figure located on a small boulder adjacent to Bear Rock. Since the other etchings are much cruder than that of the well-executed bear, it has been suggested that there might have been more than one artist. Aside from the bear, the only other figure that stands out is the "twin deer." It roughly resembles a deer head with three ears.

The petroglyphs have been dated to the Late Woodland period, one estimate placing their creation at approximately 1400 CE. It appears likely the other carvings were secondary to that of the bear, especially when we take into account the shape of the boulder (the head of the main petroglyph has exactly the same outline as that of the boulder). Moreover, the Indians native to the region possessed a deep reverence toward the black bear. These powerful creatures made it into their mythology, and a bearskin robe was central to certain religious ceremonies. Also, unlike many other animals the Indians hunted and consumed, bear bones and other remains weren't disposed of in the usual fashion. Never were they given to dogs to chew on; the hunters honored the creatures. The bear petroglyph might be an attempt to pay the proper respect to the spirits of these animals.

At least two other petroglyphs are located in the park; one is said to be a simple triangle, while another, near Spy Rock, is rumored be some type of astronomical calendar/index. Markings on bedrock appear to show constellations, with grooved lines pointing to their placement in the sky during certain times of the year. It is highly weathered and difficult to make out.

Ward Pound Ridge likely has a higher incidence of petroglyphs than other areas of the Hudson Valley due to the significant numbers of natives that once called Pound Ridge home and due to its importance in hunting. What is now Pound Ridge received its name from the presence of a V-shaped palisade used to corral game animals. According to the Dutch historian Adriaen van der Donck, teams of "one to two hundred" Indians would walk through forests and fields, shouting and banging items together to produce such a ruckus that it would cause wild animals to flee. "In this way," van der Donck recounts, "they drive a horde of game and slaughter them" at the tapered end of the palisaded structure or "pound."[20] One of these larger pounds was said to be located at the base of a nearby ridge, hence the origin of the current town's name.

A significant Native American village was located a short distance from the park. The exact location has been lost, but it is generally believed to have existed near the southern end of Indian Hill Road in the town of Bedford. Unfortunately, in 1644 it was the site of "one of the greatest massacres in North American history."[21] A company of Dutch and English settlers led by Captain John Underhill slaughtered between 500 and 700 men, women, and children belonging to the Wappinger Confederacy. Those who weren't killed in the fighting were burned alive in their wigwams. Only eight people escaped. Ironically, the village was called Nanichiestawack, meaning "a place of safety."[22] This surprise attack was done in retaliation for a series of raids the Indians undertook several months earlier that resulted in the destruction of numerous farms and the killing of settlers from Westchester to New York City. One notable fatality of the raids was Anne Hutchinson, an iconic Puritan dissident. The massacre of the Indian village was just one of many regrettable events that took place during Kieft's War, a three-year conflict that ended in 1645.

Getting There

Enter Ward Pound Ridge Reservation (Pound Ridge, NY 10576) via Reservation Road. A few hundred feet after passing the park entrance booth (make sure to obtain a trail map), turn right onto Michigan Road and follow it to its terminus and park in one of the two parking areas. The trailhead for Bear Rock is located at the southern side of the cul-de-sac near the wetland.

Follow the trail south. In a short distance, the trail branches off into three different directions. From here, consult the map you received at the entrance booth. There are numerous trails in this section of the park, and therefore many ways to access Bear Rock. Several viewpoints, Indian rockshelters, and even a cave inhabited by the infamous Leatherman, along with other interesting geological curiosities, can be visited in the southern half of the reservation. Consult the map to pick out a route that suits your interest and available time. Bear Rock is marked on the map.

Bear Rock (41.228364, -73.592801) is 1.35 miles as the crow flies from the trailhead.

4 Croton Point

Croton Point holds the special distinction of being the largest peninsula in the Hudson River, jutting to the center of the expansive 3.5-mile-wide Haverstraw Bay. Now owned by Westchester County and operated as a 504-acre park, Croton Point has a plethora of amenities. Pristine sandy beaches attract scores of summer swimmers. Paths and hiking trails that skirt the edge of the Hudson afford immaculate views of the dramatic northernmost mountains of the Palisades. And a diverse array of habitats attracts myriad species of birds, drawing birders from far and near at all times of the year. Moreover, Croton Point has sports fields, cabins for rent, a museum, and hosts the legendary Clearwater Festival each June. If that's not enough, the park boasts an extraordinarily long résumé of historic events that puts most other regional parks to shame. In short, Croton Point is one of those places that, like Mecca, must be visited at least once in a lifetime by residents of the Hudson Valley.

The human history of Croton Point dates back to at least 6,000 years ago. This is right around the time Native Americans began harvesting oysters and discarding their empty shells along the banks of the river. Over time these shell middens grew to be 3 or more feet thick in places, sometimes extending for hundreds of feet in length. Seven-inch oystershells have been found in the lowest levels. Ribbed mussels and animal bones are present here, too, but compose a very minor percentage by comparison. Radiocarbon dating of charcoal found at the bottom of one of these shell middens on the northern tip of the peninsula provided a date of habitation starting at 3900 BCE, plus or minus 200 years.

Many middens have been lost in the Hudson Valley over the years due to development, to erosion, and from farmers of the past using the shells to "sweeten" their soil, using it as a type of pH adjuster and fertilizer. Composed of calcium carbonate, shells decrease soil acidity and enrich the land.

Sunset at Croton Point.

In the past, Haverstraw Bay contained prodigious quantities of oysters, and vast reefs thrived in the shallow waters off Croton Point. Overcollection and pollution eventually led to their nearly complete extirpation until relatively recently. What's more, climatic differences thousands of years ago provided better conditions for oyster growth. When the first Indians began living on the peninsula, winters were milder and salinity was likely higher, the result of sea level differences. Today, oysters are making a comeback, the product of a cleaner Hudson. Small living specimens are now occasionally found along the shores of Croton Point, mixed among the more prevalent remains of their ancestors.

The Indians of Croton Point were of the Kitchewan tribe, whose territory extended from the Croton River northward to Anthony's Nose. Croton is derived from "Kenotin," the name of one of their sachems. It translates to "wild wind."[23]

The Kitchewan had a palisaded village they called "Navish" on the neck of Croton Point atop a 75-foot-high plateau, which is just east of the popular beach near the entrance of the park. "This site was chosen," a Westchester County historian writes, "for the purpose of protecting the fisheries and overawing the neighboring tribes." In 1899, four skeletons were found near an earthwork at the site. However, a larger burial ground was "situated near the entrance of Senasqua Neck," just southeast of the village, on the southern edge of a depression called Haunted Hollow.[24] Senasqua was the name of a marsh along the southern periphery of the peninsula. It no longer exists. The marsh was used as a landfill in the early twentieth century. Now capped, it appears as a high grassy hill on your left as you first enter the park. Based on a map that appeared in the March 1898 edition of *The Spirit of '76* magazine that pinpoints the location of several noteworthy features from the Native American era to the American Revolution, it appears that a significant percentage of the burial ground has itself been buried underneath tons of trash.

Hook Mountain visible from the southern tip of Croton Point.

On October 1, 1609, Henry Hudson and his crew, sailing back downriver after a failed attempt to locate the Northwest Passage, anchored off Croton Point. In 1645, under a stately white oak near the present-day location of the campground, a treaty between the Dutch and Indians was signed that officially ended the disaster that was known as Kieft's War. Willem Kieft, the director-general of New Netherland, early on in his career, despite the warnings of his advisors, demanded tribute payments from local tribes and began a tirade of maltreatment toward the natives. After reprisals by the Indians for what they viewed as unjust treatment by the Dutch, Kieft, in a disproportionate response, sent expeditions to massacre entire villages (see chapter 3, on the Pound Ridge Massacre).

Shortly after the treaty was signed, the first Europeans began living on the southern tip of Croton Point. William and Sarah Teller, husband and wife, settled the land and opened a trading post. Accounts of the initial settlement are scarce and often contradictory. Some historians such as Robert Bolton say the Indians gave the land to the couple, while Benson Lossing states that they "purchased it of the Indians for a barrel of rum and twelve blankets."[25] If the latter scenario, it is uncertain whether they purchased the land outright or if the payment gave a temporary title. Whatever the case, in 1682 the land was officially purchased from the Indians by Cornelius Van Bursum, who obtained a license from New York's governor to buy up Indian lands. Croton Point switched hands again in 1686, when it was sold to Stephanus Van Cortlandt. While the point had a myriad of lesser-known names over the years, the one that stuck for centuries was Teller's Point. William Teller, shortly after he began living on the peninsula, apparently "changed its name to Sarah's Point, in honor of his wife, but the public, less gallant than the husband, called it Teller's Point until lately, when the same capricious authority changed it to Croton Point."[26]

During the American Revolution, Teller's Point was the scene of many an expedition by both Patriot and British forces. The most well-known incident relates to a British warship known as the *Vulture* (associated with Major John André and his failed plot with Benedict Arnold to deliver West Point to the British). While the *Vulture* was moored off Teller's Point awaiting André's return from the western shore of the Hudson, Colonel James Livingston, an American commander at the nearby King's Ferry in Verplanck, had his men bring artillery out to the southern tip of the point and hastily constructed fortifications. The following morning, Livingston had his men begin firing on the ship. The *Vulture* sustained several hits but managed to slip downriver before being seriously damaged. It is because of Colonel Livingston's actions that André became stranded and eventually captured, averting a potentially lethal blow to the American cause (see chapter 1).

Another tale from the war relates to the American spy Enoch Crosby. For nine months during 1776–77, Crosby served as a secret agent for the Committee for Detecting and Defeating Conspiracies. Crosby posed as an itinerant cobbler and passed the secrets he gathered to his handler, John Jay. Harvey Birch, the main character in James Fenimore Cooper's novel *The Spy*, was primarily based on Crosby and his exploits. After his service for the committee ended, Crosby enlisted as a soldier in the Continental Army. It was at Teller's Point, shortly after the battle of Stony Point, that Crosby and a handful of men, through a scheme of deception, managed to capture a party of British soldiers twice as large as Crosby's detachment, without firing a single shot.

One day a British warship anchored off the peninsula and, like the story of the *Vulture,* was noticed by American forces, who determined to do something about it. At the time, Crosby and his regiment were stationed in Westchester. Crosby, in command of some men, concocted a plan to provide "a little sport for his soldiers."[27] Accompanied by six others, Crosby hurried to the western edge of the peninsula, where he put his ruse into action. He had one man parade the beach in a French military uniform, while he and five others concealed themselves in some bushes farther back. In a short time, the British aboard the ship took notice of the solider on the beach disguised as a French officer, and launched a small boat carrying eleven men to capture the beachgoer. As they neared the shore, the well-dressed American turned and flew into the woods. The British pursued and commanded the fugitive to surrender, but before they could repeat their demand, Crosby and his men jumped from the bushes and yelled with such vigor as to make it seem like half a regiment was present. Startled, and thinking themselves surrounded by a superior force, the enemy instantly surrendered.

After the Revolution, Croton Point was purchased by Robert Underhill in 1804. He established a farm that grew apples, grapes, and watermelons. The latter fruit was especially popular. During the War of 1812, Underhill found a booming market for them in nearby New York City. Watermelons were typically grown in the southern states, but because the British prowled the Eastern Seaboard, trade with the South proved difficult and unreliable. But the inland Hudson was free from British harassment and a convenient way to ship produce to the bustling city.

His sons Richard and William inherited the property in 1829. Richard continued his father's work but transitioned more to the growing of grapes, eventually turning his share of the property into a thriving vineyard that bottled 10,000 gallons of wine a year. He built an Italian villa near the southern tip of the peninsula, where a cluster of cabins overlooking the Hudson now stand. Three massive English yews that Richard planted in the mid-1800s remain. A historical marker nearby mentions that they were purchased from a nursery in Flushing, New York, for 37½ cents apiece. They are now on the New York State Historic Tree Register.

William Underhill took to the northern portion of Croton Point and set up a brickyard, exploiting the peninsula's extensive clay deposits. Like his father and brother, he also found success. The manufacturing of bricks continued until 1915, when the most profitable clay deposits were exhausted. Today, lost or discarded bricks can still be seen scattered around Croton Point, mostly along the shoreline. William's bricks are marked with his initials (WAU) on one side, while the other side bears the letters IXL, presumably meaning "I excel."

During the brickyard's operations, a small village sprung up on the peninsula. Between the workers and the owners, somewhere around fifty people inhabited Croton Point. In addition, countless workers commuted to the point each day from nearby towns on the mainland. The constant comings and goings from the peninsula set the stage for the many tales of spirits and spooks that emerged at this time, as workers shuffling home for the night passed by the shadowy scenes of battle, butchery, and burial.

Happy Haunting Ground

The area surrounding the palisaded Indian village and burial ground is reported to be haunted. The encounters were once said to be so prevalent that the spirits were known as the "walking sachems of Teller's Point," and the area in which they nightly roamed became known as Haunted Hollow. Some of the haunting is said to be derived from a fierce battle. "The early settlers of the neighborhood have transmitted the Indian story that a sanguinary battle once took place on the point between various river tribes and the Kitchawans."[28]

Charles Skinner, in his *Myths and Legends of Our Own Land*, attributes much of the haunting to white men tramping over the Indians' graves. Unable to rest, they "were nightly to be met on their errands of protest." At the palisaded village/fort, Skinner recounts, the Kitchewan "made their last stand against their enemies from the north." Chief Kenotin, or Croton, was among the men defending the settlement. He fought with an unrivaled courage and "directed the resistance with the utmost calm" despite a shower of arrows raining down around him.[29] He would not concede defeat until all his men were dead and the village was in flames. According to legend, right before the palisaded village was overrun by enemy warriors seeking the scalps of the dead, the chief called upon the Great Spirit with his dying breath to curse his foes, before collapsing lifeless into the conflagration around him.

But Chief Croton was unable to rest, and his spirit was frequently seen moving through the woods near the scene of his defeat. When a manor house was constructed nearby, he appeared one night to the owner and urged him to join the Continental Army. The owner agreed to do so, after which, Skinner says, Croton "never appeared again."[30]

Charles Hine, on the other hand, reported that the old chief had been encountered after the Revolution and often made it "difficult to lay a straight course for home." But as Hine would write in 1905, "nothing has been heard of his ghostship of late, and it may be that the materialistic spirit of the present age, which does not know a ghost when it sees one, has sent him off to some happy haunting ground."[31]

Another area of superstition on Croton Point is Money Hill, which, sadly, no longer exists. Money Hill was an island in Senasqua Marsh, not far offshore from the current public beach. It was demolished in the mid-1920s to make way for the garbage dump that now occupies the former marsh. According to a newspaper article in the *Scarsdale Inquirer* from December 13, 1924, Westchester County intended to remove the entire hill—all 55,000 cubic yards of it—and use it to widen the roadway of Croton Neck from 20 to 40 feet.

Money Hill received its name from the belief that treasure had been secreted on the island at one time. The most widespread notion was that the hidden booty had belonged to none other than the infamous pirate Captain Kidd. As ridiculous as this may sound, the newspaper article reported that "in times past, old Spanish coins and Indian implements have been found there."[32] Moreover, county officials, who planned to hire independent contractors for the work, put a clause in the contract that stipulated that if treasure or relics were unearthed by the crew, they would be forfeited to the Westchester County Park Commission. During the hill's demolition, implements of the Indians were discovered, but heaps of silver and gold coins were not.

Money Hill was also rumored to be the site of where the bodies of the dead who had fallen in the great battle between the Kitchewan and river tribes were cremated. Along with the location being haunted, stories were told of witches holding their sabbaths on the island and guarding Kidd's ill-gotten wealth.

But the telling of these tales quickly evaporated when Westchester County bulldozed the sandy hill and began dumping trash in the once-pristine Senasqua Marsh in 1927. It continued to be used as a landfill until 1986. By the time it was forced to close by lawsuits brought on by environmentalists, a hill 100 feet high occupying over 100 acres had emerged. It contains everything from household trash to industrial waste and even material contaminated by radium, a radioactive element. The landfill has since been capped and overlaid with soil. Millions of dollars have been spent since its closure to ensure contaminated leachate does not find its way into the Hudson.

Back in the day, the marsh and bay on the southern side of the peninsula were marveled at. "The bay," one nineteenth-century writer fondly recalled, "with its little islet, its miniature inlets, and its jutting points, is like a fairyland."[33] The deep bay once contained significant quantities of shad and other fish. But in 1841, a dam on the Croton River burst from an excess of moisture originating from a powerful storm and melting snows. The flood carried with it tremendous amounts of earth that instantly filled in the bay where the Croton River meets the Hudson. Today, the bay has an average depth of only around 5 feet. And as stated before, most of the surrounding marsh, once a boon for waterfowl and other creatures, has been lost.

The landfill today has new purpose. The entire hill is covered in a grassy meadow that supports countless bird species, many of them migrants. Croton Point is a convenient rest stop for many that follow the course of the Hudson in their travels. Various hawks, owls, eagles, and rare species of sparrow visit the meadow, in addition to meadowlarks, bobolinks, pipits, and more. It's one of the best birding locales in Westchester.

As frequent visitors of Croton Point have probably noticed, the peninsula is a bit of an enigma. The character of the park is constantly in flux, like the motions of night and day. It's a convergence of opposites. Peace treaties have been signed here and wars fought; crops have been reaped and garbage dumped; business has been replaced by recreation. Perhaps this is what makes Croton Point so remarkable—never static, it always has reason to surprise us.

Getting There

This Westchester County park is at the western end of Croton Point Avenue (Croton-on-Hudson, NY 10520). There are multiple parking areas along its length. Scenic roads and footpaths provide stunning views of the expansive 3-mile-wide Haverstraw Bay.

Bloody Pond & the Twin Forts of the Hudson Highlands

5

At the eastern base of Bear Mountain sits an idyllic kidney-shaped lake that for generations has been the scene of various recreational activities, from barbecuing and picnicking to boating. Even the occasional wedding takes place adjacent to its tranquil, blue-green waters. Being relatively close to New York City, Hessian Lake, as it's now called, attracts scores of city dwellers bent on spending a relaxing day in the country. On summer weekends, throngs of people crowd the walkway surrounding the lake so densely that the place resembles a bustling Fifth Avenue. It's hard to believe that such a popular spot, where smiles abound and the mouthwatering smell of delicious barbecue always seems to hang heavily in the air, was once the scene of grisly horror during the early days of the American Revolution.

For it was here on the shores of Hessian Lake, and at the nearby Forts Clinton and Montgomery, that an intense battle between British and American forces took place that left hundreds dead in the autumn of 1777.

The American-held "twin forts" were "within rifle shot" of one another along the banks of the Hudson River.[34] Fort Clinton stood atop a high plateau directly across the river from Anthony's Nose, a prominent and curiously shaped mountain. Just to the north, on the other side of Popolopen Creek, was Fort Montgomery. It occupied a superb location for firing on enemy ships making their way up the Hudson. Together, these forts' primary duty was to prevent the British from sailing up the Hudson to "harass the inhabitants" living on the borders of the river.[35] As a second line of defense, a massive iron chain that floated upon wooden platforms was stretched from Fort Montgomery to Anthony's Nose. With the forts and chain obstructing river passage, the British had no easy access into the interior of New York State.

This proved problematic when the British General John Burgoyne became surrounded by American forces in upstate New York, near Saratoga. Requiring relief, he urged General Sir Henry Clinton, who was stationed in New York City, to come to his aid. Clinton agreed, and as the historian Benjamin Lossing states, "Sir Henry prepared for an expedition up the Hudson, partly for the purpose of destroying American stores . . . but chiefly to make a diversion in favor of Burgoyne."[36] It was hoped that by invading the southern Hudson Highlands, some of the forces in siege of Burgoyne upstate would be sent to defend the area of the lower Hudson, thereby giving Burgoyne, who would thus be fighting troops of diminished numbers, a better possible outcome.

On his way up the Hudson, Sir Henry Clinton made several false invasions of Westchester to make it seem like he was going to assault the forces under the command of American General Israel Putnam in Peekskill. In reality, his main targets were Forts Clinton and Montgomery. The deception worked, and he met relatively little resistance when he did ultimately attack the twin forts. Landing at Stony Point, Clinton marched 2,100 soldiers around the back of Dunderburg Mountain at a place called Timp Pass to attack the forts from behind. Believing the rugged Highlands at their back provided enough protection, the Americans did not fully fortify the rear of the forts. In some places here, the walls were only half completed.

Making details of the battle often slightly confusing, three of the major commanders bore the surname Clinton—in addition to Sir Henry Clinton of the British, there was brigadier general and governor of New York George Clinton, likely whom Fort Clinton was named after (though he commanded Fort Montgomery), and George's brother, Brigadier General James Clinton, commander of Fort Clinton. Sir Henry was a distant cousin of the two Americans. Because of all this, the battle is sometimes aptly referred to as the "Battle of the Clintons."

Around the area of Doodletown, Sir Henry split his forces. He sent a detachment of 1,200 men under the command of General John Vaughn to attack Fort Clinton, and another consisting of 900 men to Fort Montgomery, led by Lieutenant Colonel Mungo Campbell. (In addition to British regulars, American Loyalists and Hessian mercenaries filled the ranks.) Their goal was to attack the twin forts simultaneously.

Both forts were "feebly garrisoned," having around only 600 men in total between them.[37] By these numbers, the Americans were outnumbered approximately 3:1. Such a meager garrison among forts that could hold substantially more troops (Fort Montgomery was designed to hold 800 men; Fort Clinton about half that amount) was partially the result of men being sent to General Washington to help defend Philadelphia. Also, because of Sir Henry's feints on Westchester, there was no talk of sending reinforcements to forts on the opposite side of the Hudson that were seemingly in no immediate danger.

On his way to assault Fort Clinton, General Vaughn "met with persistent opposition" near Hessian Lake, about 300 feet north of where the current Bear Mountain Inn stands. A hundred Americans under cover of an abatis (fortification of sharpened logs) gallantly resisted the invaders. They fought long and with a valiant effort but were eventually forced to retreat to the fort. Casualties were "considerable" on both sides.[38]

The fighting raged on for some time at the forts. Despite the British having far-greater numbers, according to a soldier stationed at Fort Montgomery, "they were

Bloody Pond (Hessian Lake).

many times beaten back from our breastworks with great slaughter."[39] Eventually, however, the tide would turn in favor of the British, and the forts were overrun. In a flurry of panic, men scampered down the banks of the ravine leading to Popolopen Creek, where they boarded boats and made their way to safety in Peekskill. Just before retreating, James Clinton was bayoneted in the upper thigh. He narrowly escaped serious injury or death by the blade having been deflected by a small book he had in his pocket. His brother George also made it out alive.

By the time the battle was over, around half of the American forces (300 men) were either killed, wounded, or taken prisoner. British casualties stood at about 140.

The following morning, the great chain that stretched across the Hudson was dismantled and British ships pressed north. General Vaughn would stop at Kingston, then the capital of New York, and set every single building ablaze, save one.

It was too late to be of any assistance to General Burgoyne, however. His troops were defeated at Saratoga on October 7, 1777, a day after the battle of the twin forts took place. The battle of Saratoga was a pivotal turning point in the American Revolution and helped the US gain a vital alliance with France. In order to proceed upriver, Sir Henry Clinton had to await reinforcements and formulate a plan to neutralize the Highland fortifications, and it is because of this delay that he was unable to give Burgoyne the requested help.

Along with the capture of the forts, the British seized a significant cache of weapons and ammunition, including sixty-seven unspiked cannon. The British held the forts for about three weeks before abandoning them. Before they left, they set the buildings on fire and destroyed other key features, which made it impossible for the Americans to reoccupy the forts without significant reconstruction.

A Gruesome Discovery

In a vindictive act, the British had not buried any of the Americans who had fallen during the battle. They simply stuffed some bodies into a barn, and during the conflagration of their departure, the deceased ended up half cremated. Others were tossed into the lake at the base of Bear Mountain.

In the spring following the battle, Timothy Dwight, an army chaplain, visited the remains of the fortifications. The smell of death permeated the air. Dwight, "a novice" to the horrors of war, found the foul odor "more overwhelming and dispiriting than I am able to describe."[40] He eventually went in search of its source.

> We found, at a small distance from Fort Montgomery, a pond of moderate size, in which we saw the bodies of several men, who had been killed in the assault upon the fort. They were thrown into this pond, the preceding autumn, by the British, when, probably, the water was sufficiently deep enough to cover them. Some of them were covered at this time, but at a depth, so small, as to leave them distinctly visible. Others had an arm, a leg, and a part of the body, above the surface. The clothes, which they

> wore, when they were killed, were still on them, and proved that they were militia, being the ordinary dress of farmers. Their faces were bloated, and monstrous, and their postures were uncouth, distorted, and in the highest degree afflictive.[41]

Because bodies were tossed into the lake, and the fact that intense fighting took place along its shores, what was once referred to by Indians and colonists as Lake Sinnipink was renamed "Bloody Pond." In the nineteenth century, the name would once again be changed when the Knickerbocker Ice Company began selling blocks of ice from Bloody Pond for refrigeration purposes. The company wanted something more palatable, opting to go with the decidedly plain "Highland Lake." Thirty thousand tons of ice were removed from the lake's surface each season. Eventually, the "Hessian Lake" appellation emerged and it has stuck ever since. This perhaps arose from the mistaken belief that Hessian bodies, not American, were cast into the lake. The name might also relate to the ghost stories concerning it.

In addition to the ordinary soldiers who perished that day, two higher-ranking officials also met their end during the storming of the forts. Mungo Campbell, the officer leading the charge of Fort Montgomery, was killed after his demand for the Americans to surrender was rebuffed. In retaliation for their commander's death, the British were especially brutal to the Americans afterward. And at Fort Clinton, Count Grabowski, a Polish nobleman and aide-de-camp to Sir Henry, was shot three times and buried ignominiously where he fell. Nothing marked his grave site, not even a simple fieldstone. The site is now forgotten. Dwight, the army chaplain, visited his unmarked grave and thought it "a humiliating termination of a restless, vain, ambitious life."[42]

So much death and bloodshed has left a supernatural mark on the area. The shores of Bloody Pond seem to be especially affected. The ghosts of Hessian soldiers shot down here appear to be restless on "overcast and gusty nights." One account from the late nineteenth century tells of how "ghostly apparitions, in helmets and vast riding boots, may be seen flitting across the dark bosom of the pond" and that the "whispering of commands in a strange tongue, and the rattle of ghostly sabers and harness," can be heard emanating from the battlefield.[43] Another story from the early 1900s relates how a man passing the lake after dark encountered a Hessian ghost, which then proceeded to chase him with a rusty saber, and that his life was only saved "by a sprightly pair of legs."[44]

Over the years, there have also been a number of drownings at the lake. Swimming is not permitted, but this doesn't stop many from still jumping in. Eerily, the bodies of drowning victims have sometimes been recovered just offshore, in the same spot the grotesque bodies of those unfortunate militiamen were spotted by Dwight in the spring following the battle. It has been suggested that those who don't show the proper respect at this hallowed spot may find themselves floating facedown in a watery grave. Could the spirits of the militiamen be teaching rowdy, disrespectful swimmers a lesson by pulling them under? Could the noise and bustle that now resounds along its shores be disturbing the spirits that up until recently had relative solitude and tranquility in the once-wild surroundings of the mostly uninhabited Hudson Highlands?

Cannon at Fort Montgomery.

Today, there is no trace of the battle that once raged along the shores of Bloody Pond, other than the occasional historical marker. It's lovely to visit the lake in June, when prolific arrays of mountain laurel adorn the surroundings. During such a beautiful period it's difficult to imagine the carnage that once tainted this picturesque body of water.

Fort Clinton's outer redoubt.

Those wishing to see tangible features of the fierce fighting can visit what remains of Forts Clinton and Montgomery. East of the lake, where Trailside Museums and Zoo now stands, is the former location of Fort Clinton. In the nineteenth century, a mansion constructed on the grounds by the Pell family obliterated almost all of the fort's remaining features. Only a single redoubt stands today—this is where some of the most intense fighting took place. Artifacts recovered from archeological excavations are displayed in the Historical Museum at Trailside. The famed Appalachian Trail cuts through the fort.

Fort Montgomery, a short distance away, is in substantially better condition and has been designated a state historic site. A walking tour, complete with a plethora of interpretive signs, outlines the specifics of the battle and explains what some of the structures were once used for.

As things quiet down at dusk in September and early October, near the anniversary of the battle, some say you can hear faint echoes of cannon fire reverberating off the sides of Anthony's Nose. But just as you begin to listen in, all returns to muted stillness, save the chirping of the crickets.

Getting There

Parking for these sites can be found in the spacious NYS-owned parking lot adjacent to the Bear Mountain Inn (3020 Seven Lakes Drive, Tomkins Cove, NY 10986). From the lot, walk to the north of the inn, where the white-blazed Appalachian Trail skirts Hessian Lake's (Bloody Pond) eastern shore. Picturesque and idyllic, the recreation area around the lake is filled with ample quantities of benches, picnic tables, and grills, all of which belie a grim tale of slaughter. Intense fighting took place between American and British forces here in October 1777. Several informational signboards around the lake detail the events.

To visit Forts Clinton and Montgomery, follow the Appalachian Trail as it continues east and passes under Route 9W. Trailside Museums and Zoo occupies the former location of Fort Clinton. What little remains of the fortifications can be found between the coyote exhibit and the duck pond.

Fort Montgomery can be accessed by taking a trail behind Trailside's Historical Museum. It leads to an overlook of the Hudson River, passes under the Bear Mountain Bridge, and leads down to Popolopen Creek. A suspension footbridge that spans the creek brings you to the remains of Fort Montgomery. The state historic site has a visitor center and a series of pathways with informational signage that allows for a self-guided walking tour. Parking can be found at Fort Montgomery (690 US-9W, Fort Montgomery, NY 10922).

6

Claudius Smith Den

The Ramapo Mountains of Rockland and Orange Counties are well known for their ruggedness and inaccessibility. Profoundly unsuited for development, the land has remained relatively untouched over the years. Much of it is now parkland. Preserved in the southwestern corner of Harriman State Park is a cavernous rockshelter that once served as the main hideout for the infamous Claudius Smith and his gang of outlaws. Hidden among a chain of low granitic hills that look like they've been violently smashed by a Herculean hammer, what is now called the Claudius Smith Den afforded significant protection to the gang and served as a convenient place to store their plunder after a successful raid. Today, the curious architecture of this natural rockshelter and associated winding passageways that penetrate deep into the mountainside draw the interest of history buffs and passing hikers. But what has really provided the site with a significant reputation is the tales of ghosts and unretrieved treasure that remains secreted somewhere nearby in this Land of Rocks.

Claudius Smith and his band of Tory outlaws first achieved notoriety during the American Revolution. The men engaged in a string of robberies and burglaries in the counties of Rockland and Orange, stealing mostly livestock, which they would deliver southward to the British to sell. While not commissioned by the Crown, the British did encourage the gang's depredations on the local populace.

Claudius was described as "a man of large stature and of commanding presence, possessed of powerful nerve and keen penetration."[45] He was a natural leader, and his extensive background in illicit matters made him perfect for the job that would gain him significant notoriety and lasting epithets such as the "Ramapo Cowboy" and "Scourge of the Highlands."

From an early age, Claudius was conditioned to a life of crime. His dissolute father initiated this by having his young son steal a prized pair of iron wedges from a neighbor. Claudius's father then helped him grind out a set of initials stamped onto

Horsestable Rockshelter.

them. As the years wore on and the boy's behavior in these matters worsened, his mother made an ominous prediction that stuck with him for the rest of his life. She told Claudius that if he continued on his current path, he would "die like a trooper's horse—with his shoes on."[46]

The American Revolution was a blessing for someone with Claudius's personality and skill set. In the chaos of war he found an outlet where he could not only freely unleash his black talents but make a fortune from them.

One of the first recorded instances of his criminal enterprises during the war dates to the year following American Independence. In July 1777, Claudius was arrested and "charged with stealing oxen belonging to the continent."[47] He was placed in a Goshen jail but with the help of acquaintances managed to escape and immediately resumed his operations. In addition to robbing local residents, he also occasionally attacked Washington's supply wagons, stealing large quantities of muskets.

Jesse Woodhull, a colonel in the Continental Army and a neighbor of Claudius's, had managed to attain the scorn of the ill-tempered Ramapo Cowboy and was issued a threat. Claudius brazenly told the colonel that he would steal his prized mare. That night, Colonel Woodhull took his horse from the barn and placed the animal in the cellar. Claudius was known for his daring behavior, and a threat from him was not to be taken lightly. Several days later, while in his house one afternoon, the colonel heard a loud commotion emanating from below, and seconds later, the sound of galloping hoofbeats. A glance out the window revealed a jubilant Claudius Smith riding away on the stolen horse while shouting taunts to the colonel. A friend who happened to be visiting at the time picked up a gun and aimed it at the outlaw, but just before he was about to pull the trigger, Colonel Woodhull pushed the gun aside, exclaiming, "Don't shoot; he'll kill me if you miss him!"[48]

There was good reason to be concerned that by shooting at Claudius the colonel would effectively sign his own death warrant. While there is little recorded information on the topic, legend has it that those who resisted the gang's incursions were often slaughtered in their homes. Any attempt at all to prevent the thieves from plundering meant the protestor was sure be the greeted by a volley of lead or the piercing of a knife blade. Moreover, Claudius was very vocal about making death threats, and one had in fact been directed at Woodhull (this threat was later rescinded when the bandit learned that Woodhull had stopped his friend from shooting).

One killing that has been tied to Claudius was the murder of Major Nathaniel Strong of Blooming Grove. The major, just like Jesse Woodhull, had a threat made against his life. Late one night while he was fast asleep, the gang invaded his home. The major, who was awakened by the loud entry, had time enough to grab several guns. As he confronted the intruders, he was fired upon, but the bullets missed him and he retreated to an adjacent room and barricaded himself in. The miscreants saw the arsenal the major carried with him, and realized that by storming the room, one or more of their party would likely be injured or killed. They decided to make a deal with the trapped man. They persuaded Major Strong that if he put down the guns and came out, no harm would come to him. Outnumbered, the major knew that he had little choice but to accept the terms if he was to stand even the smallest chance of surviving the ordeal. In great hesitation he placed the guns on the floor and opened the door. He was immediately shot and died almost instantly.

Despite the blatant cruelty, Claudius could be surprisingly compassionate at times. In fact, many residents of the Ramapos looked at him as a sort of Robin Hood. For instance, Claudius helped secure money for the wife of a man who had been captured at Fort Montgomery and sent to a British prison ship in New York Harbor. The soldier's wife had decided to apply for a loan from Abimal Young, a rich and prosperous, though miserly, farmer. He was a patriot and so was her husband, so she reasoned that Young would likely be inclined to assist.

In order for her husband to survive his imprisonment, it was necessary to send him money so he could pay for proper food. The rank and meager rations given to prisoners, who couldn't afford to purchase their own meals, often meant the unlucky prisoners would waste away and die.

But Abimal Young refused to help and sent the woman away from his door in tears. The news of this eventually made it to the ears of Claudius. Though he and the imprisoned man were on opposing sides, he felt pity toward the woman for the heartless treatment showed to her. Claudius then decided he would teach the wealthy farmer a lesson.

Claudius and a number of his gang visited Young at his home and demanded he reveal to them where he hid his money. The rich farmer flatly refused even after a bombardment of threats. Eventually, Claudius grabbed the man and threw him outside and proceeded to put a noose around his neck. The gang threatened to hang Young from his own tree if he didn't give up the money. Again, he refused. The group then strung him up for a few seconds and brought him down. They hoped that by showing him they weren't simply uttering idle threats, the man would be coerced into giving up his fortune. But they were wrong. Three times they hung him from the tree, the last time almost killing Young. It was apparent that the man would rather die than part with his money, and so they relented in their attack. They then proceeded to ransack his home and, after a long search, in addition to discovering several valuable deeds, bonds, and stocks, located a fair amount of hidden cash. Content with their acquisition they left, leaving the stingy farmer alive but broke. It is said that a portion of the money Claudius obtained from Young he sent to the soldier's wife, thereby enabling her to provide for her imprisoned husband.

Another time, right after the fall of Fort Montgomery, an American who had been stationed there was making his way back home. While on the road, he happened to spot Claudius at a distance, riding his way. Too late to try to conceal himself, he put on a brave face and met the outlaw. The two knew each other. Claudius was cordial and inquired about the news from the river. After a brief, and uncomfortable, conversation on the part of the soldier, Claudius said to his acquaintance, "You seem weary with walking; go to my dwelling-house yonder and ask my wife to get you a breakfast."[49] The man politely thanked Claudius and seemingly accepted the offer. But once he had ridden out of sight, the man picked up the pace and went straight home without a single stop.

Storming the Stronghold

The local citizens, tired of the gang's violent acts, finally decided that it was time to rid themselves of the Tory outlaws once and for all and formulated a plan to storm their mountain stronghold. Scouts sent out to spy on the gang discovered that the outlaws had recently made a large acquisition of cattle and horses and were making preparations to drive them to Clarkstown. An expansive rock overhang, which formed a natural barn and appropriately was called Horse Stable Rock, housed the animals at the base of the mountain where the villains resided. Since all members of the gang were present, it was determined that this was the time to act.

On a particularly dark, blustery night, a party of twenty-five men headed into the woods. They had hoped the wind would muffle their movements, so the gang wouldn't be tipped off to their presence until it was too late. Eventually, the party split into two groups to approach Claudius Smith's Den from different directions in order to surround the stronghold. As the group approaching from the south neared where the animals were stored, a blaze of gunfire erupted, shots being fired from behind the cover of trees and boulders. The outlaws had been tipped off (likely from a traitor among the would-be assailants) and were on the offensive. After a brief skirmish, the foray was deemed a failure, and those who had intended to eliminate the outlaws had no option but to retreat if they themselves were to escape from being annihilated. By the time they had made it out of the woods, one party member was dead and four were severely wounded. It is said this disastrous attempt to quell the outlaws "had the effect of making Claudius bolder than ever."[50]

Claudius Smith Den overlooking Horsestable Rock.

This boldness continued until Governor George Clinton (of twin-forts fame) stepped in. After hearing of the murder of Nathaniel Strong, Clinton put a $1,200 bounty on the capture of Claudius and $600 for his sons, Richard and James, who rode along with their father and committed similarly heinous crimes.

The bounties, which at the time were considered a small fortune, greatly encouraged the harassment of the Ramapo Cowboy. Groups of men bent on obtaining the rewards left Claudius with little time to do anything other than evade capture. Tired of being doggedly pursued, he decided to decamp to an area of British-held Long Island where he had been born.

Here he stayed for some time before being discovered by an American officer by the name of Major John Brush. Brush, who secretly crossed over to Long Island from Connecticut to keep tabs on his property from time to time, had learned of Smith's residence on the island during one of his trips. Returning to Connecticut, Brush assembled a group of four men and rowed back across Long Island Sound again. Under cover of darkness, the group hurried over to the house where the bandit was lodged. Upon entering the building, the men discovered the landlady sitting by the fire. They inquired what room Claudius was staying in, and after the frightened woman pointed it out, they rushed in and seized the sleeping man. He put up a significant struggle and attempted to grab a pistol secreted under his pillow, but it was to no avail. The Scourge of the Highlands had been captured and, after being tied up, was taken back to Connecticut and then transferred to Orange County, where he ended up in the Goshen jail once more.

Claudius Smith was put on trial and found guilty of several robbery and burglary charges. Of the murders he is believed to have committed, there wasn't enough evidence to convict, and he wasn't even tried for them. But his thievery was enough to condemn him. At the conclusion of the trial, Claudius and several members of his gang who had likewise been captured recently were sentenced to death by hanging.

Believing that the men of the gang who remained at large would attempt to storm the jail to free their leader, the sheriff ordered a guard to stand by Claudius's cell at all times. Furthermore, he made a public statement that if any attempt was made to liberate the Ramapo Cowboy, the guard on duty had orders to shoot him in his cell. No one came for him. So, on January 22, 1779, the infamous outlaw was led to the gallows.

Claudius was dressed in impeccable neatness, wearing a jacket of particularly fine broadcloth decked with large, resplendent silver buttons. It was hard to believe that someone so seemingly refined and gentlemanlike in appearance could be such a hardened criminal. It is said that thousands came out that day to watch him die. On his way to the spot of execution, Claudius tersely conversed with several acquaintances who were in the audience, one being his victim Abimal Young. The miserly man pleaded with the cowboy to reveal where he kept the important documents he had stolen. To this, Claudius replied, "Mr. Young, this is no place to talk about papers; meet me in the next world and I will tell you all about them."[51]

Shortly after this exchange of words, Claudius walked up the steps of the gallows, and just before the noose was placed around his neck he stooped down and removed his boots. This strange act caused quite a stir in the audience, and one man inquired to the condemned man why he had done so. Claudius revealed what his mother had prophesized—that he would die with his shoes on—and that he wanted to "make her out a liar."[52]

After these last words, he was hanged. While the members of his gang who were also hanged at the same time thrashed around violently, Claudius was determined to show no feeling and so hung straight down, "and scarcely a shudder passed over his gigantic frame."[53] He was buried in an unmarked grave a short distance from the gallows.

Even though the ringleader and several members of the gang were dead, the citizens of the region couldn't rest peacefully—the remnants of the gang still prowled the secluded highways, with Claudius's son Richard now running things. And Richard swore to avenge his father's death.

In March 1779, Richard and his gang killed one man and attempted to take the life of another near the Augusta Iron Works in Monroe, in retaliation of them attempting to apprehend the murderous gang. The man who was killed was taken from his home and shot in the back. The outlaws pinned a letter on the man's body, addressed to the rebels. The lengthy message declared that the gang would now begin killing six men for every one of theirs killed in the future, for the maltreatment of their late leader. They added a particularly chilling flourish at the end, stating that if the rebels continued on their current course, the gang wouldn't stop "till the whole of you are murdered."[54]

The gang continued their depredations for another three years, until the attempted murder of a well-respected citizen caused a significant outrage that resulted in the people of the region, supplemented with Continental troops, rising up to finally expel the gang from New York. By 1782, the gang was no more, and with the war finally winding down, the people of the Hudson Valley could begin to relax, rebuild, and seek the treasures the gang had hidden in the mountains.

A Different Type of Treasure

One of Smith's gang members who had been apprehended and given a prison sentence, when pressed, told of a treasure buried on a farm in the vicinity. After some searching, the hoard was found, though its contents have not been recorded. He also spoke of gold and other valuables being secreted in three caves, but these were never located. The caches are said to contain an assortment of items ranging from gold coins to silver and pewter plates to more-mundane objects such as guns. Claudius Smith purportedly boasted to his gang that he hid his personal share of the loot in various caves. Between his treasure hoards and those of his compatriots, there are likely half a dozen or more sites in the Hudson Valley that could possibly still hold the gang's ill-gotten wealth. There are tales of plunder being hidden atop Hoopsnake Hill in Sugar Loaf, somewhere among the rattlesnake-infested environs of Schunnemunk Mountain and the Shawangunks, and of course around the gang's notorious lair—the Claudius Smith Den.

Though many have searched for the treasure over the years, almost all have gone home empty handed, even those holding what one may label "treasure maps." After the gang disbanded, Richard Smith and a few other gang members escaped to Nova Scotia, where they raised families. In the first half of the nineteenth century, these descendants, equipped with written directions from family members who had hidden the valuables, attempted to locate the caches. The only items ever recovered were some rusty muskets. It's likely that a number of these caches were emptied out years earlier by members of the gang who had returned to the area. Still, there are those who continue the search today, bushwhacking throughout remote sections of the Ramapos and other purported treasure sites, searching the innumerable small caves, crevices, and other voids in the rocks that may still contain unrecovered plunder.

While the caches have yet to be located, a different type of treasure has been unearthed at the Horsestable Rockshelter. With the overhang being over 70 feet long by 15 feet wide, this rockshelter is by far the largest around for many miles. Over the millennia this exceptional spot has offered respite from the elements to countless passing Indians, colonial hunters, and other wanderers.

In 1907, a group of archeologists, hearing stories of the infamous den, decided to attempt to locate it to see what contents of history it held. But back then, like in the time of the American Revolution, it was rather tricky to find; hence why it made such a perfect hideout for the gang. Many people in the surrounding area had heard of the place, but to the disdain of the archeologists, no one could tell them where it was located. Week after week throughout the summer, they spent days bushwhacking through the wilds of what is now Harriman State Park in a futile attempt to find the elusive rockshelter. Finally, a farmer who lived 2 miles south of the landmark came forward and told the men that he had visited the site and would agree to lead them to it.

As soon as they laid eyes on the place, it was apparent that they would be rewarded for their efforts. And so, they began to undertake a comprehensive archeological examination of the site. The bottom of the rockshelter contained, at its deepest point, 2 feet of soil and was filled with numerous artifacts dating from colonial times all the way back to aboriginal prehistory thousands of years ago. In the first few inches of soil the men discovered four lead musket balls, in addition to three British coins made of copper, two dating to 1729 and the third from 1737. Deeper down, numerous relics of the Indians presented themselves to the explorers. In addition to thousands of chert flakes, the men found 158 significant artifacts. Two well-preserved spearpoints, one 5 inches long and the other a respectable 3 inches in length, were discovered, along with "eighty-nine arrow-heads, of which fifty were perfect, besides sixty-six fragments of heads and one scraper."[55] Hundreds of animal bones were also recovered, mostly of deer but also of other animals such as bear, wolves, opossum, and beaver.

While digging, the men noticed that in several places the soil appeared to have been disturbed in the past, possibly by treasure seekers. They also observed that the high presence of shattered artifacts might be a result of the livestock that were formerly stabled there by Claudius and his gang. A thorough examination of the main passageway that cut into the mountain above the rockshelter, the actual "Den of Claudius Smith," failed to reveal anything.

The narrow interior of the Claudius Smith Den.

This winding passageway is over 50 feet long and generally no wider than about 4 feet. In spots, the ceiling is 20 feet high, with massive boulders wedged between the walls of the chamber overhead. Directly above Horsestable Rockshelter, atop a set of rock slabs that look like a set of stairs, a very narrow entrance to the passageway exists. It's difficult to discern from the ground. If attacked, men of Claudius's gang could undertake a treacherous rock scramble to the top of the shelter and, after squeezing their way into the passageway like a groundhog, vanish from sight. The passageway veers southeast, leading to a spot higher up on the mountain that cannot be seen from the rockshelter. From here, it's only a short amble to the top of a high, rounded hill that affords expansive views. Gang members probably used this hill as a lookout.

Despite archeologists failing to turn up anything tangible in the passageway, a tale from the late 1800s recounts a stunning discovery made there. One afternoon, a boy of 11 or 12 exploring the site decided to poke his head into the larger entrance of the passageway on the hillside. Upon doing so, he heard what sounded like a series of clinks and scratching. He entered the chamber to investigate. To his horror, he encountered ghostly skeletons busy at work overturning rocks on the floor and pawing at crevices with their bony hands, as if searching for something. Even though the boy got within a few feet of the phantoms, they didn't pay him even the slightest notice. After staring at them dumbstruck for ten or twenty seconds, the boy gained the courage to turn and flee.

At night, strange lights are occasionally reported in the area, hovering in the confines of the rockshelter and slowly darting about in the surrounding woods and neighboring wetland. Those encamped nearby also tell of muffled shrieks heard emanating from the passageway. No one has been brave enough to investigate. Some discount the shrieks as nothing more than the sounds of animals. Others believe them to be the voices of restless souls that still roam around a site that has been used by humans for a variety of purposes over the past several thousand years.

Some say Claudius, in particular, cannot find rest and continues to visit the scenes he once frequented in life. After being hanged, the Ramapo Cowboy was interred in an unmarked and shallow grave a short distance from where he was executed. In 1841, his grave was rediscovered and his remains removed. His skull is purported to have been placed above the entranceway of the new Goshen Courthouse being built at the time. Other parts of him were said to have made it into various morbid collections, with a few bones being fashioned into the handles of knives. It seems Claudius Smith might still have the power to kill even long after his death.

Getting There

Parking for the trail that leads to the Claudius Smith Den is located at the end (cul-de-sac) of Johnsontown Road in Sloatsburg, NY 10974. From the cul-de-sac, walk south on Johnsontown Road for about 100 feet and bear right onto the blue-on-white trail. Follow the trail for 2 miles. At the trail junction, turn left and head downhill, following the red-on-white trail. Within a few hundred feet the rockshelter portion of the Claudius Smith Den (41.197782, -74.167938) will come into view at the base of the mountain on your right.

To find the cave that leads into mountainside and overlooks the rockshelter, retrace your steps and head uphill. On the left, in a couple of hundred feet, is the entrance to the passageway. Watch your head as you enter—it's a bit of a tight fit!

For a panoramic viewpoint of the surrounding Ramapos, proceed back to the trail junction and continue farther along on the blue-on-white trail as it steeply ascends the mountain. Within a minute or two, the top can be reached. This is the spot where Claudius Smith's men stood watch against intruders.

7 Stone Chambers of Putnam County

Amid the darkened, craggy, boulder-strewn slopes of various hills, mountains, and narrow hollows in Putnam County lie countless enigmatic, single-room stone structures built without the use of mortar and, in many cases, stone-cutting tools. Built into the sides of hills or partially buried underground, the "stone chambers," as they're commonly referred to, hold a grand air of mystery—no one as of yet has been able to conclusively prove who constructed them or for exactly what purpose. No other archeological sites in the region have been as scrutinized or have stirred up as much interest as these simple yet impressively constructed chambers.

Ranging in size from approximately 10 to 33 feet long, having a width of typically no more than 10 feet, and being around the height of an average person, these structures are by no means large. What makes them remarkable is the amount of effort that clearly went into their construction. A majority of the stones used in the structures are quite hefty, weighing in at substantially more than a single individual could haul. Lintels and capstones especially tend to range on the larger size, often being multiton slabs. Moreover, chambers are typically corbeled, meaning that inside walls are curved inward by a series of overlapping stones. Construction was a team effort, requiring tremendous strength, precision, and willpower. The oftentimes odd placement of the chambers, in conjunction with the labor-intensive process to build each one, has led many to scratch their heads. What's more, several chambers are aligned perfectly with certain celestial events, such as solstices, equinoxes, and the rising of constellations. And while the occasional stone chamber pops up in Dutchess or Westchester Counties, or in New England, the highest concentration (more than one hundred) of the structures is crammed tightly within the Hudson Highlands of Putnam County.

The King's Chamber.

Theories abound as to their purpose. Many speculate that these chambers are nothing more than old root cellars utilized by local farmers. Some believe them to be of Native American origin, possibly used as sweat lodges, as burial chambers, or for religious rites. Others have truly extraordinary theories that border into the far-fetched: that the structures were built by ancient European explorers before the time of Columbus for ritual purpose or as extradimensional portals. The Celts, Phoenicians, Vikings, and even inhabitants of Atlantis have all been named as possible sources over the years.

Clearly, some chambers were constructed and utilized as root cellars to store perishable food items by early farmers, but it's not entirely apparent if all that occur on farmsteads are of colonial origin. Perhaps these existed before European settlement and were converted to root cellars later on. Written reports are few and far between. If colonial inhabitants did construct them, they left little written evidence. But it must also be taken into consideration that people in the eighteenth and nineteenth centuries didn't usually write about building mundane structures, such as outhouses. Then again, something like a wooden outhouse required only a fraction of the time and manpower to build. It's a bit hard to fathom that such a major construction task would fail to be recorded time and time again in the numerous journals and letters still extant from that era.

In fact, one of the scant pieces of written evidence that does exist tends to help corroborate the theory that at least some of the chambers were in existence prior to European settlement. A 1645 letter written by John Pynchon of Springfield, Massachusetts, to John Winthrop Jr. of Connecticut reads:

> Sir I heare a report of a stonewall and strong fort in it, made of all stone, which is newly discovered at or near Pequot. I should be glad to know the truth of it from your selfe, here being many strange reports about it.[56]

The "stonewall" and "fort" (a chamber) is likely a reference to a site in Groton, Connecticut. The Gungywamp site, as it's known, contains an abundance of stone structures, ranging from stone chambers to stone circles, petroglyphs, and more. One chamber contains a "window" in one of the walls that allows light to fully illuminate an alcove in the structure on the equinoxes. There is still debate as to who the builders were, but at least part is likely the handiwork of Native Americans. John Pynchon's report indicates the site was not created by the English. At the time of his writing, New England had been settled for less than twenty-five years, and the area around Groton for considerably less. Surely, there would be some memory of who created it if settlers had a hand in the construction.

In the Hudson Valley there is no archeological data that directly points to pre-Columbian origin. But since many of these sites have been regarded as nothing more than root cellars by mainstream archeologists, comprehensive examination by means of archeological digs has not been undertaken. However, excavations in Massachusetts and Vermont have revealed the presence of Native American lithic remains (stone tools) in two chambers, as well as fragments of carbon. Carbon dating has indicated that one of these New England stone structures has probably been standing since at least 500 CE.

Then there is the controversial Mystery Hill in New Hampshire. Dubbed "America's Stonehenge," this gargantuan complex consists of standing stones, stone chambers and walls, and what appears to be a sacrificial alter. Carbon dating and the orientation of astronomically aligned stones have led some to determine that the site has been in existence for 4,000 years. Those who believe that the site is ancient are split between Native American and Celtic or Phoenician origin. Others indicate that while the area may have indeed been inhabited by aboriginal peoples thousands of years ago (based on the presence of stone tools and pottery on the site), most of structures were created during the early 1800s by a farmer and his sons for penning animals and to aid with other farmwork.

As stated earlier, some chamber stones weigh in at thousands of pounds and would have been incredibly difficult to move and maneuver without the use of powerful farm animals, such as horses and oxen. Many point to this fact when referring to them as colonial root cellars. Indeed, it's hard to dispute this, and it makes the idea that Native Americans or ancient mariners built them more than a little improbable. Still, megaliths of the British Isles—such as Stonehenge—structures far, far larger than our humble Putnam County variety, were built thousands of years ago, likely without the help of animals.

If in fact many of these structures are ancient, it would be far more likely that they were created by people known to have lived in the area thousands of years ago. The Wappinger Indians held sway over most of what is now Putnam County. Native Americans clearly had the know-how to create intricate stone structures. Just look at the Anasazi and Cahokia cultures. Respectively, they built large-scale stone dwellings and massive earthen mounds used as temples and tombs. While neither of these groups were by any means nearby, long-distance continental trade and migration routes existed, so the diffusion of knowledge related to complex engineering is possible. Obsidian projectile points, for instance, have been found in northern New Jersey. The closest naturally occurring source of this material is 1,500 miles away in the West.

A majority of structures show no modern tool markings. Many stones in the structures are completely unaltered. Some may have been shaped by wooden wedges and the use of fire to split the stone. It has even been observed that obvious drill markings don't necessarily indicate recent origin. Native Americans used flint-knapped drills to cut through solid rock. By using a bow, a drill could be quickly rotated. Sand facilitated the process. This could even be done by hand, by furiously rubbing a stick with a drill attached between both hands, in a manner similar to starting a fire. Well-known artifacts such as bannerstones, or atlatl weights, were constructed this way. While it was a painstaking process, a symmetrical hole would eventually emerge.

Those who believe that the chambers were manufactured by ancient mariners, such as the Celts, note the perfect alignment of some of the chamber entrances to celestial events. During a solstice or equinox, the sun perfectly passes through the entryway, illuminating the back of the chamber. Ancient-mariner theorists are quick to point out that a farmer building a root cellar or icehouse wouldn't go out of their way to ensure that the door was oriented in this way. Moreover, they state they have found proof to back up their claims that the Celts or some other similar culture visited the Highlands of Putnam County millennia ago. Ogham inscriptions and petroglyphs are said to dot the walls of some chambers and nearby boulders (Ogham is an ancient Celtic alphabet). A trio of slashes and even an "Eye of Bel" have reportedly been discovered at a number of sites. These supposedly represent the Celts' sun god, Bel. The markings and the chambers' orientation to important solar events are claimed as proof that the chambers were constructed and used to worship this particular deity. While some are convinced, many are not.

Those who refute these beliefs say that the so-called inscriptions are nothing more than scratches left by glaciers during the last Ice Age, or have come about from some other force of nature. A simple trick of the eye, as it were, by a mind wanting to see patterns in randomness. The chambers' alignment to the sun is curious, but it may have been a way for farmers to ensure that ample light flooded an otherwise darkened root cellar. Since no electricity existed, this would have been a clever way to aid in illumination. It's also interesting to note that no Bronze Age artifacts of European manufacture have ever been found in America. You would think that somewhere a coin, tool, or other identifiable artifact would have turned up over the years. But there's nothing.

Even if the Celts could have built these structures, you might ask, Why would they? Why would these people have traveled thousands of miles across a treacherous Atlantic in flimsy ships to build temples in the remote mountains of Putnam County? It doesn't make much sense until you think about what all seafaring nations are in quest of: trade routes or commodities. It has been proposed that the Celts, Phoenicians, or Vikings may have traveled to North America mainly in quest of resources, specifically iron and copper ore. The Hudson Highlands are rich in metal, especially iron. While pursuing or extracting their quarry, perhaps they found time to construct the chambers in gratitude to their gods for their safe passage across the Atlantic and what they discovered in this abundant land.

Personally, I feel as if the ancient-mariner theory is a bit tenuous. If indeed these structures are ancient, I'd put more weight into Native Americans constructing them. Going back to the issue of astronomical alignment, many people use this as a primary argument for postulating that only ancient European civilizations would have the necessary knowledge or drive to align these chambers with constellations and solar or lunar events. However, historical evidence indicates that the aboriginal peoples of North America were in fact quite astute when it came to observing astronomical events. In a letter written in 1524 by Giovanni de Verrazano to the king of France, regarding the former's exploration of the coast of the Northeast, he describes in great detail the habits and customs of the Native Americans he encountered. "When sowing," Verrazano noted, "they observe the influence of the moon, the rising of the Pleiades, and many other customs derived from the ancients."[57] Roger Williams, the founder of Rhode Island, wrote similarly: "They are punctuall in measuring their Day by the Sunne, and their Night by the Moon and the stares, and their lying much abroad in the ayre; and so living in the open fields, occasioneth even the youngest amongst them to be very observant of those *heavenly* lights."[58] Williams further mentions that their observation of the heavenly lights went beyond farming practices or curiosity. They find "the Sun so sweet," he writes, that "He [the sun] is a God they say."[59]

So, we have another sun god in the mix, this one a local, homegrown deity. This, along with the fact that the aborigines likely had the skill to construct stone buildings, gives more plausibility to native construction over foreign.

When we factor in Occam's Razor—the principle that the simplest explanation is most often correct—the theory that stands in the forefront is that of colonial origin. The Highlands have an abundance of easily accessible material to work with—heaps of stones are literally scattered across the hilly landscape. Moving the stones would have undoubtedly proven burdensome, but no quarrying was required and the transport of material was negligible. Early settlers cleared the land by piling the jumbled stones into walls and, likely, more-utilitarian structures that would assist with farmwork. And they would have had the easiest go at it, having had farm animals to assist with the labor and extensive experience in construction. The stone chambers were perhaps a regional motif that spread among the close-knit community of the Highlands but, through the highly isolated nature of the area, were ultimately confined mostly to the Highlands of Putnam County. Still, we are left asking questions.

The lack of proper ventilation in many of the chambers gives credence to the notion that the chambers would have been worthless as root cellars, since the buildup of ethylene gas from produce would cause it to quickly spoil. But given that the area is rather unsuited to cultivation, and better purposed for sheep and dairy farming, these may have been used for storage for something other than produce—such as milk, cheese, and meat.

Stone Chamber along Ludingtonville Road.

The interior of the King's Chamber is reputed to be a gateway to another dimension.

Maybe some were built simply more as decorative pieces, somewhat like the little nonfunctional wells and windmills people today put in their front yards. But this also raises questions: What prudent farmer would take copious amounts of time away from his busy schedule to tinker around with something that had little to no utilitarian value? Also, there's the possibility that these stone chambers were repurposed into farmers' "root cellars" upon European settlement. Some structures show modern drill marks in the upper stones, but stones in the lower layers are undressed (show no marks of having been worked). Curiously, this may indicate that aging structures were repaired and improved (more than a few contain bricks and doorjambs and have been touched up with mortar). Could some of the chambers be of great antiquity but, as a result of these modern improvements, were mistaken to be of wholly recent origin?

While the theory of colonial origin is most sound, no single theory has enough solid evidence to completely invalidate the others. We will likely never know what their exact purpose was, and so, the mystery will remain.

Strange Forces & Paranormal Activity

The chambers are said to sit on magnetic anomalies. Purportedly, these deviations in the earth's magnetic field are so strong that in at least one chamber they are able to reverse the needle on a compass. Some believe the Celts mapped the anomalies and constructed the chambers at their center. Others propose that magnetic material (some sort of metal or lodestone) was buried at the entryway of the chambers. In either case, it would be possible to find the structures with a compass and would seemingly imbue shamans or priests with magical powers when performing religious rites to an audience (such as being able to reverse the orientation of a compass). It's also possible that the magnetism may have simply served some other unknown religious purpose.

A visit to a stone chamber may affect the mind and body. Certain chambers supposedly infuse visitors with energy, making them feel elated, even giddy. On the flip side, several are said to cause a malignant drain that may lead one to feel weak and unwell for days after entering.

Paranormal activity has been reported at the chambers and in the surrounding vicinity. Malevolent hooded apparitions with red, glowing eyes; poltergeists; and small leprechaun-like creatures called pukwudgies, trickster spirits of local Native American mythology, are said to hang around the structures. One particularly bizarre encounter at the King's Chamber—Putnam's largest known chamber, located in the depths of Fahnestock State Park—even made it into a documentary aired on the SyFy Channel a number of years ago. A woman on her way to visit the chamber alone on a stark winter day recounts that during her hike out to the chamber, she encountered a shadowy, transparent humanlike figure following her through the woods. "Shadow people," as they're commonly referred to, have been recorded all around the world, clustered at certain hotspots. They are believed to be beings from another dimension that enter our world via certain portals or gateways. The unique magnetic anomalies at the chambers are evidence, some say, that they are being used as a gateway to another dimension by shadow people and others.

A high incidence of UFO sightings have been documented near the chambers. These were most numerous in the 1980s, when the Hudson Valley was flooded with the mysterious aerial displays. While UFOs aren't as prominent in the area as they once were, strange lights are still reported. Glowing orbs that dart through the forest understory and bright visual displays likened to lightning at ground level sometimes startle those who happen to be nearby after dark. Ninham Mountain, a peak said to be sacred to local tribes, contains several chambers. The lights here are thought to be Indian spirits.

The stone chambers are reputed to be used by local Wiccans and other mystics for the power they contain and to pay homage to the Celts or whatever ancient culture that they think constructed them. Burnt candles, colored feathers, dream catchers, and other artifacts of the occult are routinely encountered on the inside of the structures. It seems that the chambers draw just about everyone, from researchers intent on unlocking the secrets they hold, to curious sightseers and Hudson Valley residents, to the mystics just mentioned. Just maybe, it might not be that outlandish to think they draw a few otherworldly creatures too.

Getting There

While many of the stone chambers throughout Putnam are haphazardly strewn across the county, there are a few hotspots where clusters parallel roads, allowing for quick and easy access.

Ludingtonville Road in Holmes, NY 12531, has nine chambers, most of them visible from the roadway. The chambers are located along a 2.7-mile stretch of road between Route 311 and Mooney Hill Road. A particularly fine example, perhaps the best to be found along the road, is situated at the following coordinates: 41.501067, -73.670900.

Several chambers are also to be seen along Route 301 in Carmel, NY 10512. Two of the most prominent are separated only by a little more than half a mile. One is directly opposite the entrance to Forest Court; the other is a couple of hundred feet south of the intersection of Farmers Mills Road, on the opposite side of the road. Both chambers are only a handful of feet from the pavement.

Two chambers are located toward the end of Mt. Ninham Court in Ninham State Forest. One is adjacent to the main parking lot; the second is located slightly farther up the mountain, a short distance beyond the gate as one walks toward the fire tower.

The largest and most prized of the stone chambers is also among the most difficult to access. The 6' × 35' King's Chamber is part of Fahnestock State Park and can only be reached by following a series of informal, unmarked paths and some minor bushwhacking. Park at the end of Waywayanda Court in California Hill State Forest (dirt parking lot holds 4–5 cars). Begin your trek by following the woods road across the stream at the outlet of the lake. Coordinates of the King's Chamber are 41.420620, -73.789302. From here, using the coordinates and perhaps a satellite view of the terrain, proceed south. Follow the informal paths / overgrown roads whenever possible. You're getting close to the chamber when old building foundations and other ruins are seen scattered throughout the forest. The hike will likely be approximately 3.5 miles round trip. A smaller chamber known as "The Tomb" (41.420123, -73.788846) is located a few hundred feet away from the King's Chamber.

For directions to the Winter Solstice Chamber, see the directions to Hawk Rock.

A thorough, but not complete, listing of stone chambers in the Hudson Valley can be found by following this link: https://bit.ly/2GKVik3.

* Numerous stone chambers are in rough condition and should be approached/entered with caution. Many are located on private property.

8 Hawk Rock

Buried deep in a Putnam County forest, nearly 2 miles from any road, can be found a towering 25-foot high boulder known as Hawk Rock, perched atop a small rise in a shady, stately stand of hemlock trees. This prominent landmark is what is known as a glacial erratic. These are created when a stone is ripped from the earth and transported by a glacier until the ice melts and the rock finds itself ultimately deposited some distance from its original source. The majority of these erratics are small to moderate sized, round to oval-shaped boulders. With how numerous they are in this part of the Northeast, they are often passed by without notice. But occasionally, one of these stones is of truly gargantuan proportions and has a unique shape or placement that catches one's eye like Hawk Rock does.

The immediate surroundings boast several other similarly sized monoliths, some actually larger, such as Balanced Rock (not to be confused with another rock in Westchester with an identical name), which, as the name suggests, sits atop other small boulders. One passes it on their way to Hawk Rock. It's curious, but not as impressive a stone as one that clearly resembles a raptor. It doesn't take any squinting to see the form. The resemblance is so spot-on that some believe that it was shaped by Native Americans. It likely wasn't. However, there was undoubtedly a Native American presence in the area. The land in which the monolith stands was a hunting ground used by the Wappinger tribe, and possibly held as sacred ground. A nearby rockshelter, a natural overhang of rock that provided protection from rain and the elements, was used by the natives. And then there are the carvings in Hawk Rock.

On a flat section of the north side, where a "wing" is located, a set of carvings, or petroglyphs, are clearly visible. These figures include a turtle, a bird (now mostly gone), and a beaver or a star, depending on your interpretation. Professional archeologists have investigated the petroglyphs and believe them to be of recent origin—namely, from the twentieth century. Edward Lenik, a prominent archeologist and author of a book

Hawk Rock.

detailing northeastern petroglyphs, visited the site in 1987. In his opinion, the petroglyphs "appear to have been cut with metal tools (Lenik et al., 1993)."[60] Talking to nearby residents whose family once owned the land Hawk Rock sits upon, he discovered that a group of teens in the late 1920s were the likely artists. There are those who dismiss Lenik's findings, believing the artwork to be genuine Native American petroglyphs. Philip Imbrogno, a paranormal researcher who has spent many years investigating

Petroglyph of a beaver (or star) and a turtle on the side of Hawk Rock.

curious monoliths and stone structures in the region, told a reporter from the *New York Times* whom he took out to visit the site that the carvings are "ancient Wappinger work."[61] In an article of his own that appeared in the *Connecticut Post* in 2010, Imbrogno states: "There are historians and researchers in New York who believe that the carvings, or petroglyphs, could be more than 6,000 years old."[62]

Adjacent to Hawk Rock is an expansive table-like rock that could have been used at one time to hold council meetings or powwows by the region's aboriginal inhabitants. It's not hard to envision a group of Indians gathered on the table rock at night, conducting a religious ceremony or contemplating the prospects of war or peace beside a blazing fire dimly illuminating the lofty, hawk-shaped monolith. Fragments of half-charred wood atop the stone attest to its current use as a gathering place. Who knows what once passed at this spot centuries ago, when nothing but primeval forest loomed across an entire continent?

Hawk Rock sits in the center of a darkened hemlock grove. The heavy shade cast by the trees prevents shrubs and other vegetation from growing thickly in the understory, thereby opening the area up and providing it with a temple-like ambiance. After an hour's hike in the warm, sun-dappled woods that inevitably causes one to work up a sweat, it's a relief to stumble across the monolith and have the heat and swarms of insects dissipate. At first, the foremost feeling is refreshment, but in short time as one wanders around Hawk Rock and becomes better acquainted with its surroundings, a solemn and pensive demeanor eventually develops. It's easy to see why some consider this location sacred.

Winter Solstice Chamber.

While the area near the monolith has a very different composition than other parts of the surrounding landscape, the entire forest has a rich history. Horse Pound Brook, to the east of Hawk Rock, was once a colonial property boundary. Hefty stone walls course through the woods, especially in the area near the end of Whangtown Road in Carmel, where the access point to the property is located. Some of these walls are the largest I have seen anywhere in the Hudson Valley, with several constructed from massive stones weighing many hundreds of pounds. The remnants of a stone-and-earthen ramp that were once part of a barn are still formidable after a long abandonment. Now a young forest, the land was once occupied by a farm owned by Moses Mead in the 1860s. Three stone chambers are also on the property. The yellow trail passes by all of them, although only the "Winter Solstice Chamber" is easily visible. This is one of the most famous stone chambers of Putnam County, so named on account of the entryway lining up perfectly with the early-morning sun around December 21, the winter solstice. It's also one of the best preserved.

Once slated for development, the sacred forest and all it contains is now safeguarded from destruction. New York City's Department of Environmental Protection holds the land as a watershed buffer area. While it can be explored by the public, a permit must first be obtained from the agency. It's a simple process that can be done online, taking only a few minutes. Once the forms are filled out, you can print the permit and parking pass.

Getting There

Access to the trailhead for Hawk Rock is located at the very end of Whangtown Road in Carmel, NY 10512. A three-car parking area is on the left, immediately before the termination of the dirt road.

In order to park and hike on land owned by the Department of Environmental Protection, a permit must first be obtained. An application can be found on the DEP's website by following this link: https://a826-web01.nyc.gov/recpermitapp/. Fill out the form, click submit, and print out your free permit.

Two trails (yellow and red) form a loop through the property. Hawk Rock can therefore be accessed following either one, but the yellow trail offers more sights, such as the ruins of the Mead Farm and the Winter Solstice Chamber.

If you choose to follow the yellow trail, the trailhead can be found directly behind the parking lot. A one-way trek out to Hawk Rock is 1.7 miles. Throughout your hike a series of hefty stone walls will be seen coursing through the forest. These are remnants of the Mead Farm. In about 0.4 miles from the start of your hike, the stone foundations of a barn and other structures become visible just off the trail. Slightly past this point, on your right, an informal trail leads a short distance (100 feet) to the Winter Solstice Chamber (41.477923, -73.697383), one of the mysterious stone chambers of Putnam County.

From the Winter Solstice Chamber, continue following the yellow trail for another 1.25 miles. At the trail junction, bear left onto the red trail and follow it to its terminus in less than 1,000 feet. Hawk Rock is located at the end of the trail.

From the intersection of the yellow and red trails to Hawk Rock, other prominent glacial erratics are passed. "Balanced Rock" can be seen on the right, almost immediately after bearing onto the red trail.

For the return trip, you can continue along the red trail to complete a loop or return via the yellow trail to revisit the intriguing stone structures. Both trails are of a similar length.

9 Balanced Rock

Many things that were once mysterious and awe inspiring in the past no longer hold the same appeal they once did, as advances in science and our understanding of the natural world have provided us with answers to countless age-old questions. When it comes to the massive monolith known as Balanced Rock, a 60-to-90-ton pink granite boulder precariously propped up atop six cone-shaped limestone supports along Route 116 (Titicus Road) in the town of North Salem, the passage of time has only heightened the mystery, however. New theories and a newfound courage to question everything we've been taught about the enigmatic monolith have caused us to reexamine the case.

Until recently, nearly everyone believed Balanced Rock to be nothing more than a curious glacial erratic, all aspects of its odd placement purely coincidental. (If we recall what was said in the chapter detailing Hawk Rock, a glacial erratic is a boulder that was scoured from the landscape by glaciers, transported south, and dropped into its current configuration as the ice slowly melted.) Modern geologists dismissed any other explanation regarding its origins. And indeed the granite boulder is, without a doubt, a glacial erratic, evinced by the glacial striations visible on parts of it. But the pertinent question to ask is this: Did a glacier place it on its perch, or is its balancing act the result of actions by ancient humans?

Balanced Rock has a similar appearance to man-made structures in Europe known as cromlechs and dolmens. These standing stones were constructed by the Celts and other ancient civilizations, mostly serving as grave markers. New evidence that North America was visited by Europeans before the sailing of Columbus, such as the discovery of several supposed Viking outposts in Canada, has rekindled centuries-old theories that had generally been put aside a long time ago.

In 1824, the geologist John Finch wrote an essay in which he described Balanced rock "as a magnificent cromlech, and the most ancient and venerable monument which

America possesses."[63] While he believed that Native Americans constructed it, he thought the resemblance of the structure to those in Europe was no coincidence and "suggest[s] that the Aborigines of America were of Celtic origin."[64] We know through DNA analysis that Native Americans are of Asian origin and are not related to the Celts. But statements such as this bolstered the notion that perhaps the natives got some instruction from ancient European visitors or even that the structures were constructed by the Celts themselves. Even in Finch's day it was a common theory that Balanced Rock and other similar monoliths were completely natural. But Finch refuted the notion of it being a byproduct of nature, and strongly rallied against the belief that it was dropped in its current placement by "diluvian torrents."[65] In 1824, the idea of the Ice Age was still in its infancy, and curiously perched boulders were sometimes thought to have been a result of the biblical flood from the story of Noah's Ark.

During the nineteenth century, opinions were split between natural and artificial origin. Back then, those believing that American structures were man-made faced far less skepticism, as opposed to in the twentieth century, when a belief in any other theory than glacial origin in explaining Balanced Rock's existence was ridiculed. A British magazine in 1867 stated that "A fine cromlech still exists at North Salem, New York."[66] And in 1881, Robert Bolton, writing a book on the history of the county, records: "The rocks which serve as pedestals, have somewhat the appearance of pillars; whether fashioned by art, or the effect of accident cannot be ascertained—as time and weather would long ago have effaced the marks of the tool, had any been employed."[67]

The pillars are what most focus on today when pointing to human construction. The placement of the pillars forms a rough triangle. Apart from the decidedly nonnatural appearance of the limestone supports, a measurement of the base of the triangle reveals something astonishing. The width measures 5.44 feet, which is exactly double what is known as a megalithic yard (2.72 feet). European dolmens were usually constructed using the megalithic yard or multiples of it. This, many claim, is proof that Balanced Rock wasn't solely a product of chance.

Alternative theories that compete with the long-held view of glacial creation have gained such traction that a town sign at the site describing the monolith was recently amended to include the mention of possible Celtic origin.

Regardless of how the boulder became propped up—whether naturally or artificially—Balanced Rock almost certainly had some Native American connection. Titicus Road, which passes within 20 feet of the landmark, is reputed to have once been an Indian path. Even if they didn't have any hand in its creation, they would have taken more than a casual notice of a monolith like this. "Our native Indians," Robert Bolton says, "held them in high veneration, viewing them as holy oracles."[68] Likely some type of worship or ceremony took place at Balanced Rock periodically. It has also been suggested that it might have served as a trading post of sorts. It's a landmark that would certainly be hard to miss and couldn't be confused with any other.

Measurements taken around the site have revealed that there is a major negative magnetic anomaly below the stones. In other words, this means that the earth's magnetic field here is abnormally weak. It's curious that such a significant anomaly would be located at this exact spot. There are those who think that this anomaly

This side of Balanced Rock bears graffiti from Civil War soldiers.

Curious cone-shaped pillars support the up-to-90-ton boulder.

might imbue the area with certain special properties. Purportedly, seeds left under the granite capstone have a significantly higher probability of germinating and grow faster than those in control groups. This is similar to what is witnessed at the nearby stone chambers that also have unusual magnetic properties. In addition to enhancing fertility, Balanced Rock is reputed to alter consciousness, occasionally providing visitors with visions and tweaking their way of thinking.

The spot isn't exempt from paranormal activity. Multicolored orbs of light are said to swarm around the boulder at night. And on rare occasions, strange overhead beams of lights are seen, appearing to emanate from a hovering craft. Authorities contend that these encounters are the result of a helicopter, but witnesses claim the scene is always perfectly silent.

In addition to visible phenomena, photographs sometimes capture objects that were not seen at the time, such as balls of light and streaks of plasma. It has been theorized that the odd sights are the result of the magnetic anomalies, in conjunction with a piezoelectric discharge from the stones. Piezoelectricity occurs when a force is applied to crystals, and the stones, as a result of the applied pressure, give off electricity. In a way, the crystals are somewhat like a battery. Might the weight of the boulder on the stone pillars be stressing crystals in the granite enough to produce a noticeable electric discharge that can be seen with the naked eye or captured by a camera when atmospheric conditions are just right? Some think so.

Other happenings at Balanced Rock have no plausible explanation. Late at night, those driving past the landmark are said to sometimes see strange, ghostly figures in cloaks huddled around the boulder. Native American spirits are also said to roam the grounds. And faint, disembodied voices and chanting that permeate the nighttime air might be heard by those brave enough to approach the monolith in the wee hours of the morning.

Local residents have noticed that an unusually high amount of vehicle collisions occur on a small stretch of road by Balanced Rock (Is this caused by some unknown force, or is it the result of drivers taking their eyes off the road to glance at the monolith?). Residents also report that the stones seemingly have the power to influence the weather. When summer thunderstorms roll through town and a direct hit by the storm looks imminent, at the last possible moment the clouds inexplicably veer away from Balanced Rock, leaving the area for the most part unscathed.

In 1959, the property containing Balanced Rock was donated to the town of North Salem. The site was later designated a historic landmark. Today, there is parking for a couple of cars in front of a circa 1869 barn (also town owned), feet away from the enigmatic monolith. The only clear mark left by those who have been here before us is a set of initials and dates carved on the western face of the granite capstone by Civil War soldiers. The rest of the site is all natural—or is it?

While contemplating the landmark's origins, be sure to place a hand on the stone. Can you feel the energy that supposedly radiates from it? If you have no luck in this regard, at least you can go away knowing you've touched a piece of history.

Getting There

Balanced Rock is located at 667 Titicus Road, North Salem, NY 10560. Park in front of the town-owned barn (lot can hold two cars). The monolith is directly adjacent the barn.

10

Indian Brook Falls

At the base of a deep and secluded ravine in the craggy confines of Putnam County, where the Hudson Highlands form an indomitable rolling wall of granite that makes even a short trip seem like a wild expedition, a small brook glides among jumbled boulders and the decaying trunks of hemlocks on its way to the Hudson River. About half a mile north of its terminus with the river, a sublimely beautiful 25-foot waterfall enlivens the tranquil, low-lit surroundings. Indian Brook Falls has attracted countless visitors over the years, many of which, after glimpsing the wild grandeur of the spot, have been inspired to record the remarkable scene through paintings, verse, and prose (and now photography). Now residing on parkland, the falls are a protected treasure that will continue to offer its peaceful respite to all who require a momentary escape from the bustle of everyday life.

Flowing into a shallow cove of the Hudson, known as Constitution Marsh, the area surrounding the outlet of Indian Brook was occupied for thousands of years by Native Americans, who had a minor settlement in the vicinity. Waterfalls were sacred places to most native peoples, believing these spots were the abodes of spirits. It is therefore unquestionable that Wappinger Indians, a subtribe of the more encompassing Lenape, regularly journeyed to the falls to pray and conduct other religious ceremonies.

The falls were once simply known as "Indian Falls," but the name was later changed during the twentieth century to "Indian Brook Falls," probably to help distinguish it from the myriads of others bearing identical names across the country.

Throughout the 1800s, numerous descriptions of the waterfall and associated treks out to it were published in both books and magazines. These writings reached a zenith during the Romantic era, a period in which emphasis was placed on aesthetic experiences derived most notably from the raw and sublime forces of nature. The writings are prolifically descriptive and vivid, eliciting the same level of emotion that a mesmerizing photograph today provides. High-profile writer-adventurers, such as

Nathaniel Parker Willis and Benson Lossing, were among those who helped catapult the site to fame.

The noted essayist and author Nathaniel Parker Willis provides a singular description of the falls in his classic book *American Scenery*, published in 1840. In his opening lines he calls Indian Brook Falls "a delicious bit of nature . . . possessing a refinement and an elegance in its wildness which would almost give one the idea that it was an object of beauty in some royal park."[69] Further along in his narrative, he documents an excursion out to the falls with a group of local residents aboard a wagon fashioned in the old Dutch style. To view the waterfall required travel on a rugged and, as he would later discover, dangerous road. The road was "in some places, scarce fit for a bridle-path," and so clogged with imposing rocks "which we believed passable when we had surged over [them]—not before." Eventually, a wide and level section of the road appeared; the driver then became "ambitious" enough to push the horses into a gallop, but being "ill-matched" in strength, they jostled the fragile wagon in such a way as to detach several important features that sent the passengers flying to the floor. The mayhem was put to an end at a sharp turn in the road, where the uncontrollable horses, "unable to turn, had leaped a low stone wall."[70] After salvaging one unbroken champagne bottle from the wreck, the mostly uninjured party continued to the falls on foot and enjoyed a pleasant afternoon there.

Despite the unpleasantness of the journey before modern improvements made access easier, a visit to the falls was consistently undertaken by crowds of people of all temperaments and levels of physical ability. Though the Hudson Valley held many additional spots of attractive natural splendor, Indian Brook was described as containing "the most beautiful of its scenery." Aside from the pleasing cascade, the uncontaminated wildness of the spot drew crowds hoping to glimpse a portion of the country that hadn't yet been altered by progress and still held the same untouched features that its aboriginal inhabitants once viewed. Elsewhere in the valley, logging and farming had tamed the land and turned much of it into a quaint pastoral setting. But in the rugged Highlands, the land, as an article writer for *The Ladies' Repository* described, was "self-defended by the integrity of nature" with its "palisadoed inaccessibility," and that the "hardiest engineer will know it is not 'worth while' to delve amidst these rocks."[71] Here, people could come and romanticize about Indians and days of old in the proper setting, without having to travel to equally pristine settings out West or to the northern extremes of the state, such as the Adirondacks.

The area not surprisingly became a favorite subject with artists. Numerous paintings and engravings exist from the nineteenth century that render the locale in nearly perfect likeness and served as a simple photograph would do today in a newspaper or magazine. Others, however, show freer rein by the artist, boasting exaggerated features that are in tune with the particular inclinations and feelings of the era. The various depictions are useful for peering into the minds of the past and being able to witness firsthand the impressions the location made on these first intrepid nature seekers.

Another valued feature of the spot was its ability to act as a panacea, or restorative, to both the mind and body. "Tourists are always in raptures with the Falls," the editor

Indian Brook Falls is 0.75 miles upstream of the Hudson River.

of *Dollar Monthly Magazine* wrote in 1864, "because the sound of the moving waters is pleasing to the senses, soothing those who have tender nerves, and creating a feeling of delicious happiness."[72] In a similar vein, another advocate of the potential healing powers of Indian Brook rapturously exulted, "May the heart, the spirits, the *soul* be here refreshed and *refined*!"[73] Clearly, just as the Indians before them, the early residents of the Hudson Valley viewed powerful sites such as these in a sacred manner. The unspoiled surroundings resembled to them an Eden, and they appropriated their time there accordingly. At the base of the plunging falls is a deep, expansive basin filled with transparent water and edged with a soft, gravelly bottom, appropriately named the Musidora Pool (translated to "Gift of the Muses"), which, according to Willis, "Nature has formed it for a bath."[74] One has to wonder how many visitors over the years have cleansed themselves in the crisp water of the pool, similarly to the ablutions of a baptismal font.

Local legend dictates that lovers who visit the falls together during the evening will find themselves engaged or married by the following spring.

While during the day Indian Brook was the epitome of Hudson Valley beauty, as night overtook the already blackened ravine, the surroundings rapidly put on a gloomy demeanor as darkness and a diverse assemblage of shadows proliferated in the steep-sloped and narrow chasm. This now lonely and increasingly fearful spot became the perfect haunt for spirits. A mixture of both reverence and apprehension undoubtedly swirled around the minds of those on their way to Cold Spring or Garrison as they crossed the tiny stone bridge that spanned the brook only a short distance downstream of the falls.

Legends and ghost stories, held in distant memory, were quickly dug out from the dusty recesses of the mind and recalled in perfect detail. Unable to think of anything else, these thoughts took on a life of their own. Was the sound echoing out of the inky darkness upstream the melancholy weeping from the ghost of a jilted Indian maiden who took her own life rather than deal with the loss of her lover, or was it simply the potent roar of the falls obscured and dwindled by the wind rushing through the valley? Was the trembling figure crouched amid the bushes the protective spirit of a dog still doing his master's bidding even in death, or was it merely a prostrate log, given an animal resemblance by the pale luster emanating from the full moon overhead on a clear, late-fall evening?

The Indian Princess and the Dutchman

According to legend, during Henry Hudson's 1609 expedition up the river that would later bear his name, his ship anchored one day off Denning's Point. A portion of the crew disembarked and journeyed into the wilderness in search of food to gather. As the men were plucking sumptuous grapes from tangles of vines that overhung clumps of sassafras and witch-hazel in a sunny forest gap, showers of arrows suddenly emanated from the darkness and fell upon the group. Jacobus van Hooren was the only one hit by the projectiles, receiving an injury to the leg. Having left most of their weapons behind, the rest of the party scrambled to the safety of the ship. They left their companion for dead. Once back aboard the ship, they sailed away, leaving Jacobus to his fate among the trackless continent.

But the natives had mainly meant to scare the interlopers away. They took Jacobus back to their camp and treated his wounds. Over time, he became well liked and respected, and the tribe's chief decided that Jacobus should marry his daughter, Manteo.

The Dutchman consented to the union, seeing as he had but little choice. The wedding was set to be held in the spring, still half a year away. During the interval, the two wandered the forest hand in hand, trying to become better acquainted with one another. Often, they would sit and talk beside a small waterfall only a short distance from the Hudson. Manteo soon grew to love her betrothed. While Jacobus cared for the girl, he missed his family deeply and longed to return to his homeland.

His deliverance was soon at hand. One day while Jacobus was out hunting, the report of a gun echoed through the still woodlands. While the sound of gunfire would often repel most whose ears it reached, to Jacobus it was the most glorious sound he had heard since having been stranded, for it could mean only one thing. Following the shot to its source, Jacobus emerged on the shore of the Hudson and beheld a Dutch vessel. Without a second thought, he jumped into the river and swam to the ship, where he was promptly taken aboard and disappeared forever.

After learning of the news, Manteo became inconsolable. Nothing her father or friends could say could assuage even a modicum of the unceasing pain she bore in her heart. Shortly thereafter, her body was found at the base of the waterfall she had spent so much pleasant time at with the one she had thought loved her deeply. It appeared she had taken her own life, jumping from the top of the falls to the rocks below. However, some maintain that she died solely from a broken heart.

A Pirate's Riches

The latter ghost was said to be the mastiff of Captain Kidd. A somewhat outrageous legend claims that Kidd burned his ship in the vicinity around West Point to avoid capture by authorities. And by rowboat, he brought a portion of his secreted treasure to the mouth of Indian Brook, where he promptly buried it. Before covering it up, he killed his dog and placed the body atop the pile of gold, so that the creature's spirit would guard it until his return. He never did make it back, though, having later been seized in Boston, transported to England for trial, and finally hanged for piracy in 1701.

As crazy as it might seem to have the infamous Captain Kidd sailing through the Hudson Highlands, he did have roots in the area. He made his home in New York City and had legal privateering expeditions financed by his associate Robert Livingston. It was said that he and his crew were sailing for Livingston Manor in the upper Hudson Valley the night the ship was lost.

Numerous other legends abound as to the supposed location of his loot. Some say his ship sank at the base of Dunderberg Mountain, across from Peekskill, and most of his gold still lies beneath the waters of the Hudson. Others attest it's hidden

Strong eddies in Musidora Pool cause fallen leaves to hypnotically swirl.

on the precipitous slopes of Crow's Nest Mountain behind a massive, unwieldy boulder called "Kidd's Plug Rock." And an even more unlikely tale tells of him transporting it west to the Shawangunk Mountains, where it was hidden in a remote cave among impenetrable pitch pine barrens.

An 1880 editorial in the *Putnam County Recorder* claimed that "the dog's haunts are around the bridge that spans the chasm, just below the falls, sometimes being seen on one side, sometimes on the other." It further goes on to mention that one night as a carriage approached the haunted area at around "ten o'clock with six persons" aboard, a member of the party jokingly said, "'Now let us look for the dog.'"[75] Almost immediately after uttering those fateful words, a wild-looking mastiff materialized alongside the wagon and began to make menacing gestures. The driver, having a gun on his person, pulled it out and fired six shots into the beast. The bullets had absolutely no effect, and the phantom dog held his ground until the terrified group had quickly proceeded on their way.

Though the old bridge still stands and provides access for the curious visitor eager to view the stunning scenery surrounding Indian Brook Falls, a modern arch bridge now spans the rim of the ravine, 200 feet above the murmuring brook and farther downstream than its predecessor, keeping heavy Route 9D traffic away from the scene. Since travelers at night no longer pass by for a possible encounter with the supernatural, the area has been given a greater degree of solitude than it has seen in a long while. The tranquility and unblemished wildness, so prized by those of an earlier era, remains intact and welcomes the wanderer with the same delights first witnessed by its aboriginal stewards.

Getting There

A small parking area for Indian Brook Falls and the nearby Constitution Marsh Audubon Center is at the intersection of Indian Brook Road and Warren Landing Road (Cold Spring, NY 10516). From the parking area, walk east along Indian Brook Road for 700 feet, passing under the bridge that spans Route 9D. In another 50 feet, on the right is a small pull-off. The green-blazed trail begins here, leading to Indian Brook Falls in less than a quarter mile.

11 Pollepel Island

Slightly more than 1,000 feet off the eastern shore of the Hudson River in Beacon lies a small, 6.5-acre island. Amtrak riders racing past the rocky citadel have but moments to view the island and the mysterious degraded remnants of what appears to be a medieval castle. Such fleeting glimpses draw intrigue. On maps and other formal documents, the place is known as Pollepel Island. But it is now often colloquially referred to as Bannerman's Island, named after the man who once owned the land and erected the imposing fortress there at the start of the twentieth century. The castle-like structure was formerly used as an arsenal to store massive amounts of gunpowder, weapons, and other military memorabilia by one of the country's first army-navy surplus dealers. Before this, the island was a place of many uses. Over the years, numerous legends arose concerning it, and the island was labeled as haunted, reputed to be the stomping ground of mischievous imps and goblins, and just overall an unlucky, forbidding place.

The origin of the island's name is a bit hazy, but we know "Pollepel" is likely in reference to the Dutch word for pot ladle. The first recorded instance of this usage dates back to 1680, when the traveler Jasper Dankens records a "Potlepels Eylant" (Pot-Ladle Island) in his journal.[76] The island has some resemblance to the convex side of a pot ladle. Early Dutch explorers did have a habit of naming major landmarks after mundane objects that they resembled. Nearby Storm King Mountain was once known as Butter Hill (it appears to be in the shape of a lump of butter), and Sugarloaf Mountain, opposite it, looks like an old-fashioned loaf of sugar but was first called Hay Hill, from it also resembling a stack of hay.

Another possibility is that drunken sailors were dropped off on the island to sober up and were hauled back aboard during the ship's return trip downriver. Apparently, a pot ladle was used to extract liquor out of barrels in times past and was thus equated with inebriation. Additionally, the name could reference

The "castle" on Pollepel Island was constructed by Francis Bannerman in 1901.

a tradition where new sailors traveling up the Hudson were thrown into the river just as they approached the island and were scooped back up via a device in the shape of a giant pot ladle. It's anyone's guess as to which of these theories is correct.

And then there's the story of the lovely Polly Pell. Two men competed for her hand in marriage—Paul Vernon, a renowned minister, and Guert Brinckerhoff, a farmer and childhood friend of Polly's. One day Guert took Polly on a sleigh ride across the frozen Hudson (before the days of icebreakers, the entire surface of the river routinely froze and it was possible to walk—or ride—from one shore to the other). Concerned that the ice was unsafe for travel after hearing reports of it already breaking up in the Hudson Highlands, Paul set off on skates to warn Polly and his rival of the imminent danger. Shortly after reaching them near the center of the river, his fears proved to be realized, with large fissures quickly opening up in the ice around them. They raced toward home on the eastern shore, but before they were able to reach land, the ice had broken up to such an extent that pools of water—far too expansive to surmount—blocked their passage and they found themselves trapped on a rapidly disintegrating ice floe. Fearing that the ice they now stood on would soon give way and all three would meet a frigid end in the waters of the Hudson, Polly began sobbing and confessed to Paul that she loved Guert more than him, and asked for forgiveness. Paul was a gracious man, and to show that he understood and held no grudges, the minister married Polly and Guert on their crumbling raft. After the brief ceremony was completed, the ice floe fortuitously drifted toward a small island, where the trio were able to disembark safely. The following morning, Paul bravely swam a thousand feet to shore and sent a boat to retrieve the two stranded lovers. The island was thereafter named in commemoration of Polly Pell.

The area surrounding Pollepel Island has always proven treacherous—strong currents swirl around the island, and blasts of wind funneled up the narrow channel to the south often pommel the sail of any vessel within range of the northern entrance of the Highlands, most appropriately called "Wey-gat" or "Wind-gate." Sitting just north of Wey-gat, which is bounded by Storm King Mountain to the west and Breakneck Ridge to the east, the island served as a major landmark to mariners. Once above the island, the river widened, and smooth sailing could be expected. The Hudson Highlands were the most perilous leg of the journey. Northbound ships always breathed a sigh of relief when they spotted the island in the distance, knowing their hardships would soon come to an end.

The very first Europeans to travel the river noted the adverse conditions in the area. On the evening of September 29, 1609, a southbound Henry Hudson and his crew aboard the *Half Moon* anchored their ship not far from the island, near "the northernmost of the mountains" of the Highlands. They decided not to continue farther, afraid of what problems a night trapped among the confines of the steep mountains might present; as Robert Juet, Hudson's first mate, wrote in his journal that evening: "The high land hath many points and a narrow channel, and hath many eddy winds."[77]

A view south toward "Wey-gat" or the northern entrance of the Hudson Highlands.

The treacherous aspects of the river here are not to be taken lightly. Around the island in Cornwall Bay, about twenty-five vessels have been mapped lining the river bottom. From the shore, the area might seem calm, but it's deceptive. Even on a breezeless, sunny day, strong river currents are always present.

One notorious event that resulted in a significant loss of life near the entrance of the Highlands was the sinking of the sloop *Neptune* in November 1824. "When just below Pollepel's Island and within sight of its place of destination, and as several of the passengers were congratulating themselves that the perils of her voyage would soon be over, the vessel was struck by a sudden flaw of wind and careened."[78] A shipment of gypsum onboard tumbled over from the wind, preventing the vessel from righting itself. Within four minutes the sloop completely filled with water and sank. About thirty-four passengers drowned. A newspaper article from 1825 records that several bodies from the unfortunate incident were found floating off the shore of Cold Spring nearly eight months later.

The unlucky *Neptune* sank in a stretch of water known as Martyr's Reach. This dangerous section of the Hudson ends at Pollepel Island. Above it, Cornwall Bay widens, the mountains turn into hills, and many miles of smooth sailing can be expected ahead, continuing all the way up to Hyde Park. It is known as the Long Reach.

Superstitious sailors and adherents of Washington Irving would likely attribute the sinking to a goblin known as the Heer of the Dunderberg and his troop of imps. The Heer is described by Irving as "a little bulbous-bottomed Dutch goblin, in trunk hose and sugar-loafed hat, with a speaking trumpet in his hand." The goblin and his imp followers, which buzz through the air like a swarm of flies, are responsible for "piping up a fresh gust of wind, or the rattling off of another thunder-clap."[79] Irving recounts the story of a nameless sloop that was subjected to the fury of the Heer just as it entered the Highlands near Peekskill at the foot of Dunderberg Mountain, where it is believed that the goblin makes his home. It is here the ship encountered a powerful thunderstorm. Through the entire course of the Highlands, the sloop "labored dreadfully," the mast in danger of splintering, and the whole sloop dangerously rocking back and forth in continual danger of capsizing. The barrage continued until the vessel "passed Pollopol's Island, where it is said, the jurisdiction of the Dunderberg potentate ceases."[80] No sooner had it crossed the boundary line when the sky instantly cleared and accostment ended. The crew knew the Heer of the Dunderberg was responsible for the terrible weather, for in the midst of the attack, a tiny white hat was seen sitting atop the masthead, the calling card of the goblin.

An Island Like No Other

The first inhabitants of Pollepel Island were Native Americans, their presence attested by numerous artifacts recovered by archeologists. Legend has it, however, that in historical times the natives believed the island to be haunted by angry spirits and refused to step foot on it. Purportedly, the Dutch put this belief to their advantage, occasionally using the island as a refuge when relations between Europeans and Indians were sour and attacks seemed imminent.

During the American Revolution a cheval-de-frise was constructed by Continental forces from Machin's Battery at Plum Point to Pollepel Island. These defenses consisted of 60-foot-long sharpened logs tipped with iron that were secured in giant caissons 40' × 45' wide. The caissons were floated into place and then filled with stones and sunk to the river bottom. The submerged and slanted logs were designed to pierce the hull of any passing vessel.

But on the morning of October 15, 1777, aided by a dense fog and propitious tide, a fleet of British warships coasted over the defenses. After the fall of the American Forts Clinton and Montgomery a little more than a week prior, the most-stringent obstacles blocking their passage north were eliminated. It's hard to say exactly why the cheval-de-frise failed, but it's likely the defenses were never fully completed. Labor was being diverted to West Point to help with the construction of the Great Chain, which would stretch from the fort at West Point to Constitution Island beginning in 1778. It is also possible that American traitors or Loyalists, knowing where a narrow passage existed in the defenses to allow the passage of friendly vessels, informed the British of the weak spot.

During the nineteenth century, the island became a haven for fishermen. It was a convenient resting place, and sheds were built to house equipment. There is a report from 1884 that appears in *The Independent* that states the island was once "inhabited a few years ago by a fisherman, whose mildly insane wife imagined herself to be Queen Victoria and her husband Prince Consort."[81] Illicit business is also rumored to have occurred on the island. To avoid paying taxes, bootleggers secretly sold their liquor there and prostitution flourished. As a result, a temperance-minded woman by the name of Mary Taft purchased the property in 1888 to halt the immoral practices.

In 1900, the island was transferred to its most prominent owner, Francis Bannerman VI. Operating a successful and expanding business in the heart of Manhattan, selling arms and military memorabilia, Bannerman needed extra space to house his goods, but more importantly, he needed a safe place to store his black powder. New York officials and neighbors were understandingly nervous about tons of explosive gunpowder being stored within city limits, and therefore pushed him to relocate. Pollepel Island provided just what he needed. Its situation in the Hudson River was remote enough to address safety concerns and ideal for shipping purposes. The craggy island sits about 40 miles north of New York City. Bannerman purchased it from Taft for $1,000.

Shortly after acquiring the property, the Scottish-born Bannerman began construction of his new warehouse and arsenal, adding numerous motifs from his homeland. What eventually emerged was a veritable seven-story castle, replete with turrets, crenelated walls, and other defenses. To deter thieves and bolster the fortress's impression, Bannerman placed Gatling guns and cannons in the compound's windows. Almost none of the buildings on the property have right angles, which many believe was instituted to make the structures appear larger than they actually are. On a north-facing wall that could easily be seen by river traffic, builders embossed in massive letters the words "BANNERMAN'S ISLAND ARSENAL." There could be no mistaking who owned the island.

Bannerman eventually purchased underwater rights from New York State and created an expansive, enclosed harbor on the island's southeastern side. Despite being already surrounded by water, he also had plans to create a moat around the island, but these never came to fruition.

Then in 1920, disaster struck. The heavily fortified powder magazine, containing approximately 200 tons of black powder and ammunition, exploded. A 25-foot-long section of a wall was hurled 1,000 feet across the Hudson and landed atop the train tracks that skirt the eastern shore. Bannerman's compound was compromised, but aside from the powder magazine being utterly obliterated, along with a section of the island on which it stood, the main "castle" remained standing, though heavily damaged. The explosion was heard from Peekskill to Hudson. The blast was so great that hundreds of window panes for miles around were shattered. Bannerman's wife and her sister, along with the island's superintendent, present at the time of the explosion, were injured but survived. Local residents blamed the incident on "river pirates," who would often sneak ashore in an attempt to pilfer supplies from the arsenal.[82]

After the explosion, minimal repairs were made, and the island continued to serve as a warehouse for the business, though after the incident, much of the Bannerman operation was moved to Long Island. In 1950, the only ferry to the island sank in a squall, hindering access. Finally, in 1967, a declining business, the result of more-stringent government regulations, made the Bannerman family close the island's doors for good, selling the property to New York State. Two years later, just as plans were being made to open the island up to the public, a mysterious fire ravaged the island, turning the castle and surrounding buildings into scorched shells. The fire is believed to have been the result of arson. After this, it was decided that the crumbling ruins posed too much of a hazard, and entry to the island was forbidden.

The stretch of water north of the island was known by sailors as the Long Reach.

For nearly forty years the ruins brooded in solitude, further degrading and slowly swallowed by a tangle of vines. The Bannerman Castle Trust eventually emerged and began clearing the overgrown paths and attempted to stabilize the structures. While much has been improved, the castle and other buildings are still exceedingly frail and in danger of collapse. The winter of 2009–10 was particularly hard on the compound, with significant portions of the castle's walls and main tower giving way. It's probably best to get out there to see what remains while there's still time. It's now possible to take guided tours of the island via the Bannerman Castle Trust.

Your tour guide will likely give tales of the supernatural. The main specter said to haunt the island is that of a sea captain. During construction, Bannerman purchased old boats and had them sunk to create a foundation for a set of docks. A tugboat captain delivered his vessel to the island and, before leaving, made a request to Bannerman that the workers not sink the tugboat until he was out of sight of the island, so he wouldn't have to witness the destruction of his beloved vessel. But for whatever reason, just as the captain was getting ready to depart, the tugboat was sunk before his eyes. He cursed Bannerman for the insult and remarked that he would get his revenge. Years later, employees in a lodge constructed near where the old tugboat was sunk reported hearing the double ringing of bells. This sound is what boats use when going in reverse. Could this be the spirit of the tugboat captain attempting to extricate his vessel from the island?

In the past, when there were still residents on the island, the sound of galloping horses was heard crossing the drawbridge late at night. No horses were on the island, however. Moreover, strange whistling sounds can be heard moving across the rocky crag, but the source has never been found. Mysterious lights also sometimes appear in the castle's windows. And on very rare occasions during powerful storms, a phantom vessel can be seen lurking to the south of the island, with unintelligible shouting from the long-dead crew echoing across the choppy stretch of water. It is believed to be the sloop *Neptune*, although Washington Irving wrote about a ghost ship that haunted the lower Hudson and Highlands years before the ill-fated *Neptune* capsized.

While much of what remains on Pollepel Island is a relic of the past, and there are comparatively few serious incidents around the island now that we have sophisticated and powerful vessels to navigate the treacherous waters, the island's infamy continues to grow. Swimmers have perished trying to reach its shores, and more recently, in April 2015, a kayaker who ventured out to the island died while attempting to navigate his way back across the Hudson—some say it was accidental; others, nothing less than premeditated murder by his fiancée.

For its size, Pollepel Island has had a disproportionate amount of accidents since records have been kept. The failure of the cheval-de-frise, the explosion of 1920, the sinking of the ferry boat that serviced the island, and the fire that reduced the grand buildings to hollowed-out shells seem to be incrementally loosening man's already tenuous grip on the island. Could the string of unfortunate occurrences be the result of invisible forces at work wanting to reclaim the island for ghouls and goblins—or are they nothing more than sabotage, poor preparation, and perhaps just a bit of bad luck?

Getting There

Unfortunately, aside from group-led tours, access to Pollepel Island is restricted. Kayaking around the island is of course permitted as long as you don't actually land on it. If you want to explore the place on foot, you'll need to book a tour with the Bannerman Castle Trust. Tours are given on weekends from May to October. Boats are launched from docks on the Newburgh waterfront. Visit the Bannerman Castle Trust's website for more information: www.bannermancastle.org/index.html.

Huguenot Street (New Paltz)

Huguenot Street in New Paltz is labeled as the oldest authentic street in America. While other areas of the East Coast were settled earlier, few to no original buildings remain, and because of rampant development the sites have lost much of their quaint charm. Huguenot Street, by contrast, contains seven stone dwellings built in the eighteenth century and several additional more "modern" nineteenth-century structures, all of which are in line with one another on a relatively short stretch of road, offset from the busy thoroughfares of town. Few traces of the current century are visible—such a well-preserved time capsule exists from the peculiar nature of New Paltz's founders, the Huguenots. These French immigrants were a close-knit people whose descendants retained and inhabited their forefathers' properties for generations and ultimately, in 1894, created Historic Huguenot Street, an organization devoted to preserving the original character of the historic village.

Like the Puritans of New England, the Huguenots came to the New World seeking religious freedom. Originally from France, this group of Calvinist Protestants found themselves increasingly unwelcome in a Catholic-dominated country, whose leaders, in an attempt to snuff out what they viewed as an expanding plague of Protestantism, relentlessly persecuted all those associated with the movement. Eventually, the Huguenots sought refuge in Germany in a region known as the Palatinate or Pflaz (Paltz). But even here, the refugees weren't safe. The French king repeatedly invaded the Palatinate, and, in 1664, one of his generals horrifically massacred the province. Amid fears for their safety, most of the remaining Huguenots decided to give up on war-torn Europe and settle across the Atlantic far away from the bloodhound zeal of tyrants.

Knowing that the Dutch were particularly tolerant, many decided to settle in the Dutch-founded colony of New Netherland (later to be rechristened New York when Britain usurped control). Most of the Huguenots eventually made their way

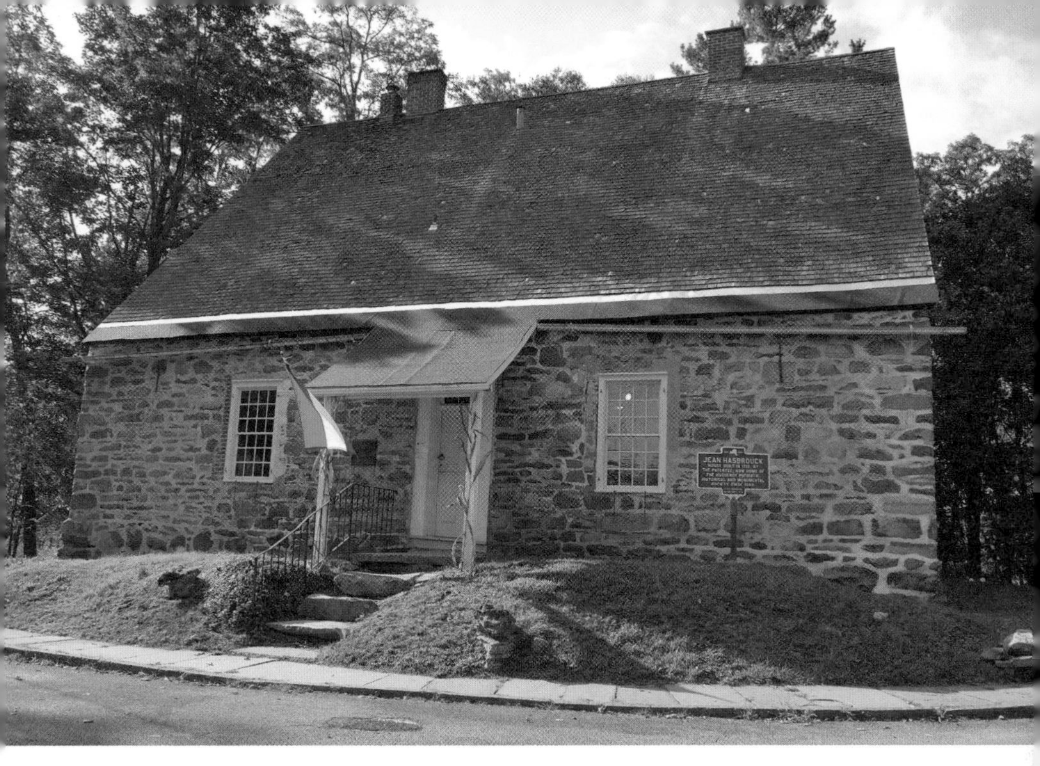

The Jean Hasbrouck House was built in 1712.

to what is now Kingston and Hurley from 1660 to 1675. Not long after their arrival, according to one historian, they began to "long for a settlement of their own where they might speak their own language and form a community by themselves."[83] This was likely facilitated by the fact that Kingston, originally a thriving trading post, was beginning to move away from the fur trade as pelts became increasingly scarce, and thus, to support themselves, the town's inhabitants were forced to increasingly rely on farming for income.

Louis DuBois, one of the earlier arrivals to New Netherland, and the eventual leader of the New Paltz settlement, knew just the spot to relocate to. In 1663, during a raid on Kingston by local Indians, Louis's wife and three children were kidnapped and taken to the Indians' "castle" or stronghold near the Shawangunk Kill. Three months after the attack, an expedition was organized to free the prisoners from captivity, Louis DuBois among one of the men involved. It was during this trek to free his family that Louis first became acquainted with the lowlands of the Wallkill Valley as his party marched across its fertile plains.

In 1677, as relations moderately improved between the colonists and Indians, he decided it would be the perfect spot to settle and cultivate the land. And so, Louis DuBois, along with eleven other men, later known as "patentees," embarked on a mission to purchase land from the Indians. They succeeded in negotiating the sale of 40,000 acres from the local Lenape tribe that included "all the present town of Lloyd, about two-thirds of New Paltz, one-third of Esopus, and one-fourth of Rosendale."[84] They purchased this by giving the Indians 400 fathoms of wampum (a form of Indian currency made of shell beads), in addition to utilitarian items

French Church burial ground.

ranging from knives and axes to kettles, gunpowder, and horses. To give legitimacy to their purchase the twelve men applied for a patent, which the British governor at the time, Edmund Andros, granted in September 1677. The price of the patent was a yearly payment of five bushels of grain to the Crown.

In the spring of 1678 the patentees and their families traveled to the banks of the Wallkill River and began construction of their new settlement. They named the placid river they settled along after the Waal, a distributary branch of the Rhine, and by adding the suffix "kill," a Dutch word for stream or river, we get Wallkill. The site they chose had previously been occupied by Native Americans. (Recently, a replica of a wigwam was installed next to where archeological excavations have shown one formerly stood.) The settlers at first built wooden houses surrounded by a palisaded fort. About thirty years later, these temporary structures were superseded by many of the fine stone homes that are still standing today. The first settlers all lived on Huguenot Street.

Despite the settlers being of French origin, their houses show many classic examples of Dutch architecture, from front-gabled facades and casement windows to jambless fireplaces. An original of the latter feature is still to be seen in the Jean Hasbrouck House, built in 1721. Remaining examples of this unique fireplace are exceedingly rare nationwide. A jambless fireplace has no sides, just an expansive hood elevated far above the hearth. The design was rather inefficient—often, smoke and ash escaped into the room, especially if it was a windy day with downdrafts. Still, with the fireplace having no sides, it afforded the often-cramped quarters a little extra space. Bricks were imported from Holland to be used in chimneys.

The homes have a storied past. State historic markers scattered around the street give terse tidbits of some of the more interesting history or unique architectural components. Cockfights took place in the kitchen of the Abraham Hasbrouck House. The Bevier-Elting House has a rather odd subcellar that was used as sleeping quarters for slaves. And the DuBois Fort, a residence, has gunports in some of the walls—supposedly created in fear of an Indian raid.

As previously stated, the owners of the properties on Huguenot Street were keen on keeping things in the family. Ralph LeFevre, a descendant of the patentee Andries LeFevre, published a very detailed history of New Paltz in 1903 and recorded some of his own experiences: "In the house in which I was born my father lived before me, my grandfather spent his days there, my great-grandfather dwelt there. A few rods off my great-great-grandfather's house was built."[85] Some homes were passed down in the same family for two centuries. Nowhere else in the Hudson Valley, or the country for that matter, have descendants been so involved in the familial estates of their ancestors.

Franklin D. Roosevelt was descended from Antoine Crispell, the first patentee to come to America. Crispell was transported to what is now New York City aboard the *Gilded Otter* (also the name of a popular New Paltz brewery on Main Street), arriving in June 1660. Roosevelt visited New Paltz numerous times and once toured Huguenot Street with Crown Princess Martha of Norway. Martin Van Buren, another New York president, who happened to live in Columbia County, made a trip to New Paltz with Washington Irving in 1821 to examine an old set of documents.

Also singular in nature is the form of government forged by the twelve patentees. These men ruled New Paltz as a single body, which eventually became known as the Duzine (Twelve Men). The community retained the tradition of twelve men occupying the reins of government for almost 150 years until its dissolution in 1824. Eventually, members—who needed to be descendants of the original patentees—were yearly elected to serve on the board. When first established, the Duzine had full control over the settlement in all matters, but as the years passed, their power slowly dwindled until finally they only had the authority to settle land disputes. This community government had no parallel in colonial America.

All but two of the patentees are buried in a small graveyard adjacent to the French Church located toward the southern end of Huguenot Street. Abraham DuBois was the last surviving patentee—he was interred here in October 1731. He is the only patentee with an original grave marker, formed from a rough piece of fieldstone and rudely inscribed with his name, date of death, and "Survivor of 12 Patentees." The graveyard was closed in 1864. However, in 2013 it received the burial of a slave unearthed on the property of the Deyo House around 1894 during renovations. Only a skull was found, which at the time was believed to be of Native American origin. The skull was placed in a box and forgotten about for decades. Eventually, it was analyzed by anthropologists at SUNY New Paltz, and it was determined the skull actually belonged to an African American, presumably a slave of the Deyo family. The identity of the slave remains unknown; the gravestone is marked with "Sankofa," an African word that means "it is not taboo to go back and fetch what you forgot."

Murder & Ghostly Apparitions

In September 1801, the peaceful and devout village was rocked by one of the most brutal and shocking events ever to occur in New Paltz. Along Springtown Road, opposite Huguenot Street on the western side of the Wallkill, Maria Deyo, the wife of a descendant of one of the patentees, for seemingly no reason at all, brutally murdered three of her young children and then killed herself. A newspaper article titled "Horrid Murder and Suicide" appearing in the *Guardian; or, New Brunswick Advertiser* recounts the chilling events.

One day after breakfast concluded, Maria sent her family out of the house with the exception of the three children "which she had designed for destruction." She persuaded her husband, Josiah, to go visit a cornfield to make sure vandals hadn't damaged anything, and gave a son an errand of picking up a hat in town, instructing him to take his toddler-aged sibling along. Shortly thereafter the mother instructed the remaining older children—a 9-year-old boy and a girl of 7—that she was going to comb their hair. The girl went first, with the mother telling the son that he should go out to the yard and play in the meantime. Maria then took the daughter to a backroom, where she let down the window curtains "and with a razor cut her throat from ear to ear."[86]

The disturbing events were overheard by the boy Maria had sent to town to fetch a hat. Apparently, unknown to his mother, he had decided to wait for his brother so they could go on the errand together, and sat outside on the doorstep. He heard the girl utter, "Don't, mama," to which the mother sternly replied, "Hold your tongue," followed by a faint scuffle. The boy on the doorstep didn't think much of it at the time. Then from the house, Maria called the other son who was playing in the yard to come inside, and proceeded to "comb his hair."[87] But the son put up more of a struggle, and a loud commotion could be heard emanating from the room. This alarmed the boy, and he then recollected that in the morning he had seen his mother conceal a razor beneath a piece of cloth. Now fearing the worst, he grabbed the toddler who was with him, turned from the house, and ran toward the road. Almost as soon as he had made it to the road, his brother emerged from the house with blood pouring down his neck. After running a short distance, he collapsed, dying a short while later.

The first to enter the house was the husband of one of Josiah's daughters from another marriage. He walked into a most gruesome scene—mother, daughter, and infant were found lying in a pool of blood, all with their throats slit.

The motivation behind Maria Deyo's terrible deed was never determined, although it was conjectured that it was possibly the result of "mistaken religious fanaticism." She was described as "devoutly religious, practising prayer every night with her family . . . apparently happy and contented in her family—was highly esteemed in the neighborhood, and had never discovered the least trait of insanity."[88] Her actions shook the small community and left everyone wondering why such a seemingly normal and pious woman would commit such heinous and damning crimes.

The act was clearly premeditated for some time. Two days before, another daughter, who, before leaving town for a short trip, expressed to her mother that since she had little to do at home, she would like to be absent for a few days. Maria retorted, "You will have enough to do on Monday." The daughter inquired what she meant. The mother wouldn't say but reiterated that she would have "enough to do." From these statements "it is supposed she alluded to the burying of the dead."[89] What's more, when a chest in the house was opened to gather linens to prepare the bodies for burial, it was discovered Maria had laid out a perfect number of shrouds for the occasion.

While probably the most sensational event in the town's history, the Deyo family massacre is far from the only tragedy to hamper the town. Murder may have been uncommon, but the possibility of facing an agonizing death was not. Prior to the advent of modern medicine, disease and childbirth frequently took the lives of people of all ages. Huguenot Street is littered with a plethora of dreary tales related to these topics.

The other Deyo House, located on Huguenot Street, is reportedly the most haunted of the original structures. One spirit said to haunt the premises is that of Gertrude Deyo. A portrait of hers still hanging in the house shows Gertrude as a frail, sickly-looking young woman. The 20-year-old died in the 1840s, suffering from consumption (tuberculosis) while pregnant.

Many old gravestones possess whimsical soul effigies.

When the house was recently redecorated, the portraits of Gertrude's parents, which once hung happily next to the portrait of their daughter, were moved downstairs. Shortly afterward, Gertrude's portrait began to repeatedly fall from its once-secure perch. In addition, it was sometimes found at the opposite end of the hallway, facedown. These mysterious happenings continued until Gertrude was reunited with her family.

A brief newspaper article from 1842 states that Phebe DuBois, wife of Thomas DuBois, committed suicide by cutting her own throat with a razor. One has to wonder if she got inspiration from Maria Deyo. Interestingly, the DuBois Fort is supposedly haunted by a headless woman that walks the halls during the witching hours. Could these two individuals be one and the same?

Another DuBois suicide took place in 1931 at the Bevier-Elting House. After Hugo Freer died of appendicitis, his lover, Annie DuBois, decided that she couldn't live without him and promptly disappeared. She was later found at the bottom of the well that can still be seen at the Bevier-Elting House. She is said to roam the property in a white nightgown and is often heard sobbing, presumably for her long-lost lover, and perhaps for her own untimely death.

One of the most unsettling spirits of Huguenot Street inhabits the Abraham Hasbrouck House. A man in colonial-era clothing carries an ax on his shoulder and wanders the outside of the property before being seen to enter the house through the front entryway. He is followed by a large black dog. While the man doesn't display a noticeably malevolent demeanor, the fact that the figure is seen carrying an ax might possibly allude to some egregious sin needing atonement. Who the spirit might be remains a mystery.

The oldest street in America, it appears, also happens to be one of the most haunted. Some of these tales and many others are yearly retold during evening "Haunted Huguenot Street" tours given in October. The fall is perhaps the best time of the year to wander around the National Historic Landmark District, although the nonprofit Historic Huguenot Street offers tours of the buildings and grounds year-round. It makes a large difference knowing that the Huguenots themselves fashioned the bulk of what you see. It's captivating to walk through the same doorways these intrepid pioneers once did centuries ago as they began to create a nation that, like their resolute dwellings, still boldly stands.

Getting There

Most of the homes and other buildings created by the founders of New Paltz are located toward the southern end of Huguenot Street (approximately 54–100 Huguenot Street, New Paltz, NY 12561). Tours are given regularly in the National Historic Landmark District by the nonprofit Historic Huguenot Street. For more information, visit their website: www.huguenotstreet.org.

13 Sam's Point

At the southern tip of the Shawangunk Ridge is a promontory that stands high above the surrounding country, offering wonderful views of the Hudson Valley and beyond to all who make the ascent. When the humidity is low and the air clear, mountain ranges in five states are visible. The Native Americans who once inhabited the area referred to this spot—just about the highest piece of land in the Shawangunks—as *Aioskawosting*, which means "it wears the buckhorns from across the way."[90] In other words, this mountain promontory is chief of the Shawangunks. Rising above all others, it stands supreme among the mountains. Today, we simply know it as Sam's Point, now part of Minnewaska State Park.

Who was Sam and why was a section of this lofty cliff named after him? To get to the bottom of this, we must travel back to 1758, to the middle of the French and Indian War. Back then, this was the frontier, and border warfare was common among the sparse community, which abutted a primeval wilderness. Beyond the farms and settlements hid legions of Indians trying to hold on to their rapidly dwindling territory. And the French, allied to many tribes of the region, would occasionally sweep south from their strongholds in the north and west in an attempt to secure the riches of the North American continent for themselves. While the French posed little direct threat to those near the towns of Mamakating, Ellenville, and New Paltz, nearby Indians would often engage in surprise raids to retard the westward expansion of colonial settlers.

Over the years, Samuel Gonsalus, an adept hunter and scout and lifelong resident of the border community of Mamakating, contributed to the war effort in an unofficial capacity. While out in the wilderness on a hunt or other errand, he often heard word of impending massacres devised by hostile bands of Indians, and by quickly warning his neighbors of the plots would foil the Indians' best-laid plans. He also frequently joined in expeditions against them. In this way, Sam accumulated scores of enemies bent on his destruction.

Portions of five states are visible from Sam's Point.

Lake Maratanza.

But Sam proved to be "too wary for even the wily Indian." Every ambush and trap they set for him he meticulously avoided or managed to escape. However, in September 1758, his luck was about to change. While hunting by himself atop the Shawangunk plateau near Lake Maratanza, he encountered a fast-moving "scalping party."[91] This group of Indians had recently attacked New Paltz and killed several settlers. In retaliation, they were now being pursued by a mob of vengeful townsfolk. Upon recognizing Sam, the Indian war party sent out a booming war call and set out on a chase to annihilate the one who had caused them such anguish over the years. Sam, who easily recognized that he was significantly outnumbered and stood

little chance of surviving a direct confrontation, dropped his gun and ran in the opposite direction. It must be noted that Sam was a swift runner, and there was hardly a man—white or Indian—who could out race him.

As Sam dashed away from his pursuers, he began formulating a plan of escape. He had traversed this land for years and knew every part of the terrain in great detail. With the Indians close on his heels, he headed to an overhang at the edge of a 90-foot cliff that stuck out like a massive tongue. Here he stopped to face his pursuers, who stood but a few hundred feet away. Upon seeing Sam trapped between them and the cliff, the Indians thought they had finally achieved what none of their race had been able to do in the four long years since start of the war—end the life of the renowned Indian fighter. They slowed their pace and savored the moment, eagerly seeing what Sam would do. He had but two choices: toss himself off the cliff and die a quick death or be captured by them, after which he would be most cruelly tortured.

In short time, Sam turned back toward the cliff and, after taking a brief glance below, launched himself over the edge into a sea of green that stretched into the distant horizon—down he plunged into its shadowy depths. This was no suicide attempt, but a leap of faith. He directed himself toward a clump of hemlocks that grew out of fissures on the sheer cliff face 40 feet below. Fortuitously, he landed in the intended spot and, apart from a few nasty scrapes and bruises, was unharmed. After a second of composure, he clambered down a tree, and finding the necessary supports to scale the remainder of the cliff, he safely made it back to the ground.

The Indians approached the edge but could see nothing. Assuming he was mangled on some rock below that was shielded by leafy boughs, they departed, not having the time to check to see if he was in fact dead, so closely were they themselves pursued. Much to their dismay, they later found him very much alive and as fierce an adversary as ever.

And from this incredible exploit, the landmark that locals called "the nose of the Aioskawosting" was rechristened Sam's Point.[92]

One author, however, has an alternate theory. In his book *A History of Sullivan County*, James Quinlan points out that on an old map in his possession, a tract of land near Sam's daring jump is labeled as the Gonsalus Patent. He wonders if Sam owned the land, and because of this, the now-famous promontory "was literally Sam's Point."[93]

Like Sam, and possibly because of him, the Gonsalus family was targeted by the region's aboriginal inhabitants. Sam's nephew, Daniel Gonsalus, at the tender age of 5 or 6, was captured by Indians and remained with them for three years before he was finally able to make his escape. Elizabeth, another young relative, was seized on her family farm and taken into captivity at the age of 7. Elizabeth's father refused to give up hope of her return. In great danger to himself, he tirelessly searched and made inquiries among local tribes to track her down. After twenty years, he was finally successful in his pursuit and brought his long-lost daughter, whom many had considered dead, home.

Sam's father also makes it into regional lore. Manuel Gonsalus, one of the first residents of Sullivan County, was supposedly a prospector and miner. At the time, many were confident that the Shawangunks contained stores of silver and gold (though we now know lead is just about the only ore here). A mysterious mine shaft that penetrates approximately 515 feet into the incredibly resistant Shawangunk conglomerate near Ellenville is reputed to be named after the Spaniard. The primitively hacked "Spanish mine" has been the subject of speculation for centuries. Some say the name refers to early Spanish explorers who, seeking the fountain of youth, endured months or years of toil to create the curiously dug shaft. A spring that emanates from the back of it was said at one time to contain the purest water in the world. A bottling company was eventually set up and extracted the immaculate water, making a tidy fortune. To date, no one has been able to definitively prove the mine's origins, but evidence does suggest, or at least alludes to, the possibility that Manuel may have had a hand in its creation in the early 1700s.

The spot that Sam Gonsalus purportedly jumped from to escape a hostile band of Indians.

Sam died of natural causes in 1821 at the age of 88, having escaped unscathed from all major conflicts he would find himself constantly immersed in. He had managed to survive the French and Indian War and numerous attempts on his life by renegade Indians, as well as the American Revolution. Records indicate that during the Revolution, Sam sided with the British and, somewhat surprisingly, fought alongside the famous Mohawk leader Joseph Brant.

A Journey into One of Earth's "Last Great Places"

Today, Sam's Point welcomes a steady stream of visitors, not so much wishing to see the spot of Sam's infamous jump but, rather, the remarkable views and scenery Sam's Point Preserve has to offer. The Shawangunk Ridge in this location is a plateau that's unlike any other in the world. Before transferring the land to New York State, the Nature Conservancy designated Sam's Point as one of seventy-five "Last Great Places on Earth."

Sam's Point contains more than thirty rare plant and animal species, among them the beautiful rhodora and intimidating timber rattlesnake. Moreover, it hosts the best example of a dwarf pitch pine ridge community known in the world. Stunted by a lack of soil, nutrients, and moisture, most of the pines stay well below 15 feet in height. While the occasional chestnut oak or other tree pops up, the site is overwhelmingly dominated by pitch pine. Also present in significant quantities in the understory are huckleberries and blueberries. So many bushes are present that the spot at one time was harvested by professional berry pickers who seasonally lived on the ridge in rustic huts and cabins. The dilapidated remains of these structures can be seen in the western half of the preserve.

The unique white stone that is the hallmark of the ridge can be likened to a time capsule. Before what we see today was cemented into conglomerate, the noticeable coarse sand and gravel that studs the surface of the stone, giving it a rough exterior, formed the bottom of ancient braided rivers that flowed before the first dinosaurs emerged. Of a more recent era are marks left behind by glaciers. Due to the incredibly resistant nature of the stone, we can actually see the exact direction of the ice's course. In most other areas of the Hudson Valley these marks have long since eroded or are buried under prodigious amounts of glacial till. Where the stone has been planed and polished, giving it a sheen similar to a countertop, striations in the stone made by debris trapped under the ice record the glacier's progress. Even this sky island that rises to almost 2,300 feet in elevation was buried beneath a towering wall of ice.

What makes Sam's Point so remarkable is a marvelous interweaving of history, ecology, and geology. Near sunset, the place takes on an unspeakable softness and beauty, cloaked in a myriad of pastel colors. From the edge of Sam's Point, one can see the High Point monument in New Jersey, the Kittatinnies and Poconos, and the Berkshires and Taconics, not to mention glimpses of the faraway Green Mountains of Vermont. Closer to home, a glance southeast reveals the course of the majestic Hudson and the wide gap that separates Storm King Mountain from Breakneck Ridge, forming the northern entrance to the legend-laden Hudson Highlands. Finally, looking to the west we see the sun slipping behind the sawtooth outlines of the blue Catskills, the land of Rip Van Winkle. Like Sam, this place helps you escape your problems. Just try not to plummet off the edge of a cliff while doing so—you might not be as lucky as our famous daredevil.

Getting There

At the parking lot of the Sam's Point Preserve section of Minnewaska State Park (400 Sam's Point Road, Cragsmoor, NY 12420), take the Loop Road east. Follow the road until you reach the top of the Shawangunk Ridge, at which time a junction (0.6 miles from the start of the hike) will come into view. Bear left and follow the road/trail for a short distance until the overlook is reached. This promontory is the spot that Sam Gonsalus reportedly jumped from in the mid-1700s to escape a hostile band of Indians. Aside from the history of the location, the view is remarkable, especially in autumn as the leaves change color.

From "Sam's Point," retrace your steps to the junction and bear left, once again following the Loop Road. The road passes by the crystalline Lake Maratanza in three-quarters of a mile and will eventually bring you back to the parking area (2.35 miles from the junction). The Ice Caves Trail, a spur off the Loop Road, is worth visiting if time allows. A series of caverns you can walk through are naturally refrigerated, holding snow and ice at their base sometimes until June or even early July.

14

Dover Stone Church

Compared to a "cathedral of medieval times," the Dover Stone Church, a natural and picturesque cavern carved slowly through the ages by a sparkling mountain brook cascading down the precipitous slopes of West Mountain in Dover Plains, has attracted and inspired all who have made a pilgrimage to this revered spot for as long as records have been kept.[94] Acquired by the Town of Dover in 2002 after a flurry of ownership over the past three centuries, the property was promptly transformed into parkland, allowing the community full access to this stunning natural landmark and its surroundings. Several miles of hiking trails now crisscross the well-used preserve, highlighting the exquisite beauty of the western Taconic Mountains.

Situated at the bottom of a deep ravine about half a mile distant from the busy Route 22 that bisects the town, the sides of the tight gorge the Stone Church is wedged between are covered in thick, verdant beds of moss, ferns, and other lush arrays of mountain herbage that's reminiscent of the Catskills or Adirondacks. Access to the natural curiosity remains essentially the same as it did in 1877, when a visitor documented that "a short and easy pathway, cut at the foot of a rocky declivity and along the margin of the brook, leads to the door of the Church."[95]

At the base of the mountain, as one first begins to enter the ravine, cool breezes of air can typically be felt issuing from its shaded confines. The temperature drop is quite sudden and severe. It is these qualities—the shade and temperature differential—that allow for snow and ice to linger here weeks longer than in surrounding areas. The unique microclimate supports an interesting spread of vegetation.

The ravine is shaped like a wide V, and on the north-facing slope, the one the trail passes along, thick beds of moss, usually soggy to the touch, mingle with prostrate mats of Canada yew and trees of hemlock, striped maple, and sweet and yellow birches. Ferns, too, are everywhere and even cling to sheer rock walls wherever a crack is large enough to support a few spindly roots.

The Stone Church has hosted numerous engagements and weddings over the years.

The opening of the cavern is burrowed into a vertical wall of tough metamorphic rock. The entrance resembles a "mouse hole" chewed through wall molding, though of a much-grander scale, standing 20 feet high. The interior is spacious and surprisingly well lit, and though the stream runs through the center of it, enough rock covers the bottom, similarly to a loose cobblestone road, to allow unimpeded access. During the drier months, the inside is especially easily traversed. At the very back of the main room, where the stream penetrates through the cavern, a small waterfall cascades to the left of a massive slab of rock appropriately named the "Preacher's Pulpit." Because this passage is situated almost directly due west, in the afternoon, bright, sunny rays filter through the narrow fissure in the ceiling, illuminating the spray and dust of the chamber and transforming the drab surroundings into a scene as glorious and spectacular as any found in a man-made church with panes of stained glass; hence its given name.

The rock of the Dover Stone Church, according to one geologist, is said to be "composed of garnetiferous mica schist."[96] Pick up a stone from the streambed and you're likely to spot tiny, dark-reddish-brown beads protruding from the rock, which have a dull metallic sheen. These beads are small garnets. They can also be found on their own with little effort in the sand of the stream, having been eroded mostly intact from the softer parent material.

View from the interior of the Stone Church.

A large waterfall once cascaded down the precipice that the cavern now sits at the base of. Initially, the waterfall was situated about 300 feet downstream but migrated to its current position as it eroded the rock beneath it. Right around this time, at the top of the falls, a deep crack developed in the streambed, and as rushing water, sand, and small fragments of rock swept along it, the crack enlarged, eventually forming the Stone Church. As the commodious cavern was being born, the once-mighty waterfall—somewhat similar in appearance to Awosting Falls at Minnewaska State Park—withered away as the ravine deepened and the water was redirected. The crack, now a conspicuous fissure, can be seen in the ceiling of the Stone Church, toward the back of the cavern. The Stone Church was created at the end of the last Ice Age, as tremendous torrents of glacial meltwater raced through the ravine. The current flow is but a trickle compared to what formerly plunged down the mountainside thousands of years ago.

One of the first historical references to make mention of the Stone Church dates to around June 1637. Sassacus, the sachem, or chief, of the Pequot tribe of Connecticut, reportedly took refuge in the cavern with a small band of followers to escape attack by another tribe of natives.

Sassacus had originally been forced to flee westward from the area around New London, Connecticut, when his people were attacked by the English. They hid briefly in a swamp in Southport but were soon discovered, and most of Sassacus's followers were either massacred or taken prisoner; only about a dozen escaped. The small band continued to press east and entered New York. Upon passing through Dover Plains on their long retreat, the group was unfortunate to encounter a hostile hunting party of Mohegans. After a fierce battle in which the Pequots had just managed to avoid annihilation, they retreated once more, this time to the craggy confines of the nearby Stone Church, where they remained hidden for a week until the Mohegans departed.

Sassacus, once the ruler of numerous tribes lying between the Thames and Housatonic Rivers, ultimately met an ignominious end a few months later, far away from the land of his people. The Pequots sought asylum with the Mohawks in upstate New York. But fearing the weapons and vengeance of the English, the Mohawks decided instead to seize and execute him and his warriors. The Mohawks sent the sachem's scalp, along with other severed body parts, to the English leaders as a token of goodwill.

By the 1830s, the Stone Church was a well-known natural feature, and myriads visited annually. The proprietors of the Stone Church Hotel, located only 100 yards from the cavern, recorded in 1832 that from June 1 to December 1, "there were about eleven hundred visitors."[97] Throughout the remaining years of the decade, the numbers increased even more. An article from 1838 in the *Poughkeepsie Casket* eloquently advertised the importance of undertaking a pilgrimage to the landmark, equating it to a sacred site worthy of deep reverence. The Stone Church, the author writes, "is admirably calculated to inspire the contemplative mind with devotional feelings, and to lift the thoughts of the great ARCHITECT of the universe, beside whose works the pigmy creations of proud man are merely atoms."[98]

Asher Durand, a renowned artist of the Hudson River School, journeyed to the Stone Church in 1847, making a sketch of the scene he found at hand. And Benson Lossing, a writer and Hudson Valley historian, who lived up on Chestnut Ridge in Dover, published a pamphlet describing the cavern and its environs in 1876.

Numerous adventurers of the past have left their marks upon the interior of the Stone Church. In many spots along the lower walls can be found historical, and now, unfortunately, modern graffiti. Names and dates meticulously chiseled into the resistant stone date back to the mid-1800s. One detailed individual from 1873 even went so far as to record the time of day. While these historical scribblings add a bit of intrigue to the scene, it's important to not further despoil this remarkable place by the addition of contemporary marks.

As can probably be surmised, based on the beauty and natural splendor of this sanctified cavern, the Stone Church has hosted numerous weddings over the years, as well as engagements (the author chose this site to propose). Its proximity to town, in addition to the path that leads up to it being relatively level and traveled with ease, endows the Stone Church with ideal qualities for hosting nuptials. It's difficult to envision a more perfect wilderness locale for such a union.

Few people realize that there's a waterfall directly beyond the Stone Church, rising to perhaps 30 feet. Situated farther upstream, in the wilder and more-treacherous confines of the ravine, Sassacus Falls, as it's known, dashes over colossal chunks of rock detached from the steep walls, now jumbled and haphazardly strewn in every direction in the narrow streambed. Reaching this place is arduous, and though it's possible to gain a perfect glimpse of the falls, it's nearly impossible to physically reach it. Sassacus Falls plummets into a circular pit as deep as the falls are high, with no clear route to climb in or out of. In years past, access was relatively easy—instead of having to ascend the steep slopes of the ravine and circle behind the cavern to obtain a look, a wooden ladder adjacent to the Preacher's Pulpit inside the Stone Church led to a narrow passageway that gave access to the basin Sassacus Falls tumbles into. Additional ladders on the slick walls of the ravine near the waterfall made climbing in or out of the pit possible. They have all been removed or rotted away long ago.

This carving was created by David and Joseph A. Maher, members of a prominent family in Dover Plains in the latter half of the nineteenth century. *The History of Dutchess County*, published in 1909, records Joseph as having been "the first and only boy from the parish of Dover Plains who ever embraced the priesthood." After graduating from Fordham University in 1876, "he spent four years in Rome where he was ordained priest."[6] Twenty years later, in 1893, David would return to the Stone Church and make another carving, but this time without his brother. Father Maher suffered an untimely death in 1886.[99]

Following the brook farther west (upstream) reveals several additional smaller waterfalls and cascades. A quarter-mile trek will bring you into a stately grove of old-growth eastern hemlocks.

With trees towering to heights well over 100 feet tall and having trunk circumferences massive enough to escape being fully embraced by even the largest person, these giants are easily several centuries old. Hemlocks are capable of attaining an age of over 800 years. This species has one of the longest life spans of any tree in the Northeast and happens to be extremely slow growing, sometimes taking 250 or even 300 years to reach full maturity. They do exceedingly well in shade. Growth can actually be inhibited, especially in seedlings, by direct sunlight. Stands of old-growth forest, especially when it comes to hemlock, are exceedingly rare in the eastern US, most trees having been logged long ago for lumber or the tannin-rich bark that was used to process leather.

Recently, the hemlocks of the preserve have become infested with the invasive hemlock woolly adelgid, a deadly, invasive insect accidentally introduced from Japan. While these minute beetles are often difficult to spot, their fuzzy white egg cases laid on the bases of needles are readily visible. While the infestation is still relatively minor, this is likely to change. The only thing keeping them in check is the winter cold—much of the population freezes to death when temperatures drop a few degrees below zero. But since winters of the future will be warmer, the infestation will expand. Moderately to heavily infested trees usually die within three to ten years after initial infestation. These majestic trees managed to escape the ax yet still may succumb in the future to a pest not much bigger than the head of a pin; felled not by human might but, rather, by human stupidity.

The preservation of the Stone Church, in contrast, demonstrates remarkable prudence. The many conservators and agencies engaged in making the purchase of this treasure possible must be applauded for their dedication. There are few other natural wonders in Dutchess County steeped in as much history and legend as this. The Stone Church and its tranquil surroundings are sure to soothe the tired minds and bodies of all who sneak away from the modern world and its many distractions. Now that it's protected, the Dover Stone Church will uninterruptedly be able to offer the same sense of awe and comfort it provided to the first visitors, going three centuries back to the time of Sassacus and his band of weary refugees.

Getting There

Ample parking can be found at the Dover Elementary School (9 School Street, Dover Plains, NY 12522) when school is not in session. Alternate parking is allowed at the Tabor Wing House (3128 Route 22), Fresh Co. 22 (3156 Route 22), and Four Brothers Pizza (3189 Route 22). From the school, cross Route 22 and walk north for 250 feet until the blue-and-yellow Dover Stone Church historical marker comes into view. Immediately turn left, following the narrow lane to the trailhead. From here, it's an easy 0.4 miles to the church.

15 Wilderstein Petroglyph

A charming historic estate overlooks the Hudson River in Rhinebeck. To most, the gem of the property is a nineteenth-century, thirty-five-room, Queen Anne–style mansion that sits atop a gently sloping hill. Droves of the curious interested in architectural design or those simply wanting to get a glimpse of the "finer things" visit the mansion each year. Very few, however, see what "Wilderstein" was named after. Translating to "wild man's stone" in German, the Wilderstein estate acquired its name from a petroglyph that's etched into a rock outcropping poking out of the mud in a small cove on the edge of the property. It's arguably the greatest extant Native American petroglyph located in the Hudson Valley.

Unlike other petroglyphs in the area, which can be hard to find, see, or discern, from the often-ambiguous nature of the artwork, on warm summer days when the boulder is mostly dry and mud free, the Wilderstein petroglyph requires no squinting or guesswork to identify what the carving depicts. The upper half of a human figure is clearly visible. What look like antennae sprouting from the man's head is likely a symbolized headdress, indicating this is a chief or shaman. What's more, the left hand holds what appears to be a pipe. The right hand is missing due to exfoliation of the rock, but records indicate it once held an ax or tomahawk. In a way, it's similar to our nation's seal of an eagle grasping an olive branch in one foot and a cluster of arrows in the other. Such designs represent the delicate balance of peace and war.

The petroglyph sits toward the bottom of a boulder-like outcropping that is situated in Suckley Cove, 50 feet from the shoreline. The cove was cut off from open water by the Hudson River Railroad in the 1840s and has since been filling in as a result. A thick cattail-filled marsh now occupies the almost entirely landlocked cove. The torso of the figure rests on the marsh's muddy bottom. It may extend farther below the surface.

Petroglyph of an Indian chief or shaman.

A similar though more intricate design of a man holding a gun once graced an outcropping just across the river in Esopus. It was carved into a soft shale, almost all of which has since eroded, thereby leaving the Rhinebeck petroglyph as the finest example of native art around.

In addition to the human figure, letters are reputed to be carved on the top of the rock. Some sources indicate that they are the initials "AR." One examination in 1979, however, noted that the letters consisted of "a capital A, a small s, and a backward capital B."[100] Unfortunately, a heavy coat of lichen now completely obscures the letters, so contemporary examination is not currently possible. Perhaps both sets of initials are present.

The 12' × 8' outcropping greatly stands out in the marsh and was likely even more prominent centuries ago, before the cove was separated from the Hudson by the railroad. The initials indicate that the outcropping might have served as a boundary marker. In 1686, two tracts of land constituting a total of about 2,200 acres along the eastern shore of the Hudson were sold to settlers by local Native Americans.

Suckley Cove is now mostly cut off from the Hudson River.

The petroglyph is located on the northwest face of the outcropping.

The purchasers of the two separate tracts petitioned the Crown for legal recognition of their new acquisitions. The tracts abutted one another. Two years after making the deals with the local Indians, a single royal patent covering both land purchases was granted to Arie Roosa, Gerrit Artsen, Jan Elton, Hendrick Kipp, and Jacob Kipp. The first three men owned the southern tract, while the latter two individuals owned the northern tract. According to the historian Edward Smith, "The lands conveyed by it [the patent] lie between Landsmans and Rhinebeck creeks and the river, and extend from Vanderburgh's cove north to a line drawn directly west from Hog bridge to the river."[101]

The land tract sold to Roosa, Artsen, and Elton extended from Vanderburgh's Cove north to a small creek known to the Indians as "Quanelos," later renamed "Sleight's Kill." The land that Wilderstein now occupies was once part of the tract owned by the trio. This is of importance because if the stone does indeed bear the initials "AR," they are almost certainly related to Arie Roosa. In 1710, Roosa is recorded as having sold off part of his land to Henry Beekman. This transaction involved "several marked trees and stones" bearing the initials AR and HB.[102] The outcropping in Suckley Cove may or may not be related to the 1710 land transfer, but it clearly shows that Roosa had the habit of marking stones with his initials. It is, therefore, conceivable that Roosa, at one point or another, waded into the marsh and chiseled "AR" into the stone marking his property.

The trio divided their land into six lots, each man receiving two in an alternating pattern. The mansion sits on property owned by Elton, while Roosa owned property just to the south. It's possible that the dividing line between the two lots ran east to west of the outcropping in Suckley Cove. Property records from this time are a bit shadowy, especially when it comes to delineations.

Remarkable similarities exist between the Wilderstein and Esopus petroglyphs. Both figures were carved with nearly identical antennae-like headdresses and possess similar body morphology. Moreover, both are holding something at the end of an extended arm. The petroglyphs were pecked rather than incised. And the land on which the petroglyphs reside belonged to the same tribe.

The carving of the Indian in Esopus has been shown to mark the northeastern property boundary of the 1677 New Paltz Patent. The firearm in the image proves without a doubt that the petroglyph was created sometime after 1609, the date of the first recorded European visit to the area. We are not so fortunate when it comes to dating the Wilderstein petroglyph. But based on the similarities between the two carvings, it is likely they were created around the same time. It's possible the Wilderstein petroglyph is older, but due to the shallow nature of the peck marks and volatility of the Hudson, it's unlikely that it would have been able to hold up to the elements as well as it has if it proved to be carved centuries earlier. When we compare the carving today with images taken during the 1930s, some significant deterioration is visible. This, in conjunction with the fact that initials are also present and that the outcropping falls near the boundaries of a colonial-era land sale, like that of its neighbor across the river, makes me lean toward the idea of it being of more recent origin. I think it's safe to say that the two petroglyphs are closely contemporaneous with one another, and not that the Wilderstein petroglyph dates back to 1100 CE as some have proposed.

The land sold to Arie Roosa, Gerrit Artsen, and Jan Elton belonged to the Esopus Indians, who were part of the larger Lenape tribe that encompassed much of southern New York and New Jersey. From what we know, the Esopus Indians traditionally occupied the western shore of the Hudson River in Ulster County, while the Wappinger tribe, also Lenape, occupied most of Dutchess County. The Rhinebeck / Red Hook area also sat near the territorial boundary of the Lenape and more northern Mahican. Scholars have debated endlessly over the last two centuries as to whether Rhinebeck was mostly under sway of the Lenape or Mahican. E. M. Ruttenber in his *History of Indian Tribes of Hudson's River* placed the boundary at the Roeliff Jansen Kill, a river that runs along part of the border of Dutchess and Columbia Counties. Recent scholarship has tended to place the Mahican farther south of this line, however. It's likely that most of Rhinebeck was inhabited by the Sepasco Indians (Mahicans) during the time of European settlement. The Esopus Indians owning part of Rhinebeck complicates things, but it's important to note that tribal bounds were constantly in flux, especially after Europeans arrived. By introducing a brew of disease and conflict, the settlers further shifted these already fluid bounds.

It's worth noting that the Lenape and Mahican tribes are both part of the Algonquin family and so are closely related. As far as we can tell, they were mostly cordial with one another, and villages of both tribes near the border often overlapped. In most instances, there were no clear or rigid dividing lines like we are familiar with today when it comes to property bounds.

Roosa and the others purchased the southern tract of what would ultimately become the 1688 Rhinebeck patent from Aran Kee (also known as Ankony), Kreme Much, and Korra Kee. These individuals occupied a high status among the Esopus Indians and were either tribal leaders themselves or closely related to them. The price for the land was "Six buffaloes, four blankets, five kettels, four guns, five horns, five axes, tens kans of powder, eight shirts, eights pairs of stockings, forty fathoms of wampum, or sewant, two drawing knives, two adzes, ten knives, half anker rum, one frying pan."[103]

The Beginning of the End

One apocryphal story goes that shortly after Henry Hudson's 1609 expedition, a group of newly arrived settlers asked the Indians for a seemingly modest gift—as much land as an ox hide would cover. The request was granted without hesitation. Since the Europeans' arrival, the Indians had been treated kindly by the strange men with pale skin, and they themselves were the recipients of generous gifts, such as farming implements, articles of clothing, and various trinkets. The Indians were awed by the new arrivals and looked upon them as sort of demigods. After all, these men sailed up the river in a floating village and possessed all types of marvelous instruments. They thought nothing of granting a bit of land to friends, especially a plot as small as this.

And so, the ox hide was cast onto the ground. One settler grabbed a knife and began cutting the hide into thin strips no wider than the small finger of a child's hand. In this way, the man cut up the entire hide, careful not to sever the strips and cutting the hide in a sort of spiral fashion. Once the task was complete, the heap of rope was stretched out until it encompassed a sizable piece of land. The Indians were surprised by the wit of their new friends, but not wanting to quarrel over a bit of land, they said nothing.

For a time, the two groups lived happily together, "although the whites asked from time to time, more land of them and proceeding higher up the Mahicanituck [Hudson]." Unfortunately for the Indians, they came to discover that their friends "would soon want all the country."[104]

In less than a century after the royal patent was granted to Arie Roosa and the others, nearly all the natives of the Hudson Valley would be dispossessed of their homeland. As the years wore on, tribes often had little choice but to give in to the demands of settlers. If they didn't willingly sell their land, whites would often find an excuse to take it by force. But even in formal transactions, tribes frequently found themselves cheated. Settlers sometimes had the habit of greatly expanding the boundaries of land sales after negotiations had been completed. Indians who had been wronged occasionally fought back in court. Sometimes they prevailed in their cases. But the tide was against them, and they slowly lost control of the land their ancestors had occupied for over ten thousand years. Today, little remains to attest of their presence aside from the occasional subsiding earthwork, petroglyph, or other stone feature. And even these will one day fade away, leaving only a handful of corrupted place names on a map to remind us that they ever existed here at all.

Getting There

To access the trails of the Wilderstein Historic Site (330 Morton Road, Rhinebeck, NY 12572), park in a small lot near the Gate Lodge. There are three driveways for the estate; enter the northernmost one (look for the "Wilderstein Trails & Lodge Parking" sign). The grounds are open from 9 a.m. to 4 p.m. year-round. For a trail guide and other information, visit http://wilderstein.org/.

At the western end of the parking lot, follow the trail downhill for less than a quarter mile. Once at the bottom, take the first right and briefly follow the trail to the edge of Suckley Cove. Straight ahead, about 50 feet into the marsh, is a conspicuous boulder-like outcropping (41.891814, -73.943638). The petroglyph of the human figure is located on the stone's northwestern face, just above the waterline. Wear muck boots and visit during low tide.

16 Bash Bish Falls

Hugging the border of New York and Massachusetts lies a raging cataract sequestered in a steep and rugged yet sublimely beautiful ravine. The unusually titled Bash Bish Falls is Massachusetts's highest waterfall, rising to 60 feet. Located in the extreme southwest of the state, it's easy for residents of New York to make a day trip, many of whom, despite its technical presence in New England, classify it as a natural landmark of the Hudson River Valley.

There are conflicting reports of how this waterfall came to be named. Some say it's so called due to a supposed Indian witch being executed at the spot, her name being Bash Bish. The other, more believable, explanation derives, according to a nineteenth-century author, "from an Indian onomatopoetic name," or in other words, garnering its name from the sound that falling water makes.[105] In any case, it's certainly a unique name that most people are not likely to forget (with the exception of possibly reversing the order of the words).

Before the colonization of the continent by Europeans, Native Americans undoubtedly visited the falls regularly, since these sites were believed to be the sacred abodes of spirits, a place to commune with the other side. The only direct evidence that attests to their reverence for the place is a Mahican legend, if it is indeed genuine and not something crafted during the nineteenth century by Romantic-style writers. The sad tale tells of multiple deaths occurring at the waterfall by supernatural forces (the story is appended at the end).

When this sequestered spot became relatively accessible in the 1800s upon the introduction of the railroad, crowds of curious visitors would make the trip up from New York City to spend a day in the charming Taconic-Berkshire range. Numerous magazines and traveler's handbooks made mention of the area and, of course, the famous waterfall. "Bash-Bish . . . is one of the finest points of observation between New York and Montreal," the author of *Health and Pleasure on "America's Greatest*

Bash Bish Falls has attracted many famous visitors—among them Henry David Thoreau, Henry Ward Beecher, and John Frederick Kensett.

Railroad" stated.[106] The nearby station at the Copake Iron Works allowed passengers to disembark, walk up the winding road to the falls, and be back in the metropolitan bustle of the city by nightfall. Despite the proximity of the falls to the station, one guidebook warned that "one requires a good foot, a strong hand, and a clear head" to those unaccustomed to the ruggedness of the area, which was significantly more extreme before the aid of modern roads and an improved trail system.

Several publications also urged or, at the very least, described in vivid detail wild expeditions through parts of the upper ravine that park officials today would most likely discourage for safety concerns. One of the most sought-after features was that of the "Eagle's Nest." This lofty viewpoint, a "blackened crag," towers "more than three hundred feet into the air" and "broods over the abyss."[107] The journey up it was recorded as "perilous in the extreme" by one intrepid adventurer in the 1850s, who also recalled that "scarce a foot-hold could be obtained, and we clung to the straggling plants in terror as we went."[108] Despite the difficulty of reaching the spot, an unrivaled view emerged of the ravine and surrounding countryside. Standing on the edge of the precipice and looking down toward the falls, the people below resembled the miniature "Lilliputians of Gulliver's Travels."[109]

"Profile Rock," a rock edifice resembling the face of a man, and the "Look-Off," another viewpoint of "high rocks on the south bank of the gorge," adjacent to the "Eagle's Nest," attracted additional visitors seeking an adventure.[110]

Apart from the impressive height of the falls, what's really eye-catching about the scene is the titanic boulder that sits at the very edge of the cliff and diverts the flow of the raging brook. The water is divided as it tumbles over the edge and then powerfully reunites into a single powerful stream again just before entering the swirling, emerald-tinted plunge pool, which "seethes and boils and bubbles like a great cauldron."[111] Its elegance supersedes other waterfalls of the region.

And like the unusual gap in the brook caused by the island-like boulder, the narrow ravine briefly disappears below the falls, expanding into a spacious glen—a fortunate feature that enhances the scene and allows nature's remarkable handiwork to be adequately viewed. Crowds can gather in the natural amphitheater to simply take in the view, to photograph, and, in years past, to paint, all while enjoying ample space to freely move about. The heavy mist that exudes from the falling water is refreshing on a hot summer's day as it's gently blown this way and that by the fragrant mountain breezes that sweep down the ravine, similarly to the cool flowing water of the foaming brook.

Over the years, many have compared the beguiling intensity of the spot to the forces of magic. These "fairy falls" and surrounding countryside, endowed with Elysian qualities, seemed too surreal to simply house common arrays of wildlife, such as squirrels and deer. Rather, fanciful imaginations populated the region with supernatural entities, from phantoms of Indian myth to "fairy queens" that lived in "elfin palaces beneath the earth" imagined by nineteenth-century Romantics.[112]

Enraptured visitors were often at a loss of words. "I feel the paucity of description for delineating such scenery," one professor unabashedly admitted.[113] Another "longed for the language of a poet" in an attempt to express his elated emotion. And yet others felt the scene was practically indescribable. Not content that the current words of the English language would do it justice, one adventurer wished that "someone would invent a new vocabulary" for the purpose.[114]

And there were those who required no words to convey Bash Bish's grandeur. Painters flocked to the falls in substantial numbers throughout the 1800s. The artist John Frederick Kensett of the Hudson River School produced perhaps the finest rendering in 1865. The painting shows a darkened glen with summer storm clouds amassing overhead, adding yet another layer of wildness and intensity to the scene.

Other notable individuals who paid homage to Bash Bish included the abolitionist and clergyman Henry Ward Beecher, along with the transcendentalists Henry David Thoreau and William Ellery Channing. "I would willingly make the journey once a month from New York to see it," Beecher wrote.[115] While little documentation survives of Thoreau's visit, the prolific writer did make a brief mention of it in his work *A Yankee in Canada*. This set of falls made an obvious impression on him; when he spoke of "interesting" waterfalls of the Northeast, he noted only two: Kaaterskill Falls and Bash Bish.[116]

The entire area surrounding the ravine is ideal as a botanical hunting ground. Numerous uncommon to rare plant species are scattered along the brook and throughout the nearby forests. The combination of shade, dampness, and a variety of soil types has resulted in the presence of rare mosses, orchids, and other flowers. The unusual conditions provide key habitat for species that would otherwise be absent in the more typical forest regimes of the region.

Little rivulets that continually stream down the cliff-like slopes that encircle the plunge pool feed mats of plush mosses that densely coat the rock. On a typical day, water drains off these mats like water streaming off the hair of someone just exiting the shower. One enterprising botanist had enough luck with finding rarities here that she wrote an article for inclusion in a botanical journal, titled "Rare Mosses of Bashbish Falls."

In May and June, one traipsing through the upper end of the gorge may be fortunate enough to stumble upon small clusters of the wild purple clematis (*Clematis occidentalis*). This delicate flowering vine is often found in open light twisting around riparian trees or clinging to talus or rock ledges imbued with a hint of calcium. Orchids populate the shady forest interior, adding bursts of yellow, pink, and purple to the drab leaf litter of the understory.

Before the introduction of a deadly exotic fungus in the early 1900s, impressive specimens of the American chestnut once graced the mountains here. "Chestnut formed a good percentage of the lower level growths and yearly yielded large crops until the disease made its appearance," Sereno Stetson wrote in the botanical publication *Torreya* in 1913. "These beautiful trees," he continues, "two to three feet in diameter, are now decaying masses."[117] While these mammoth and stately trees that provided tasty nuts to the area's wildlife and people alike no longer rise into the upper reaches of the canopy, traces of them can still be seen. Some roots from infected trees have survived, and it is not uncommon to see resprouts. However, as soon as they emerge aboveground, the fungus once again begins its insidious attack. Chestnut trees nowadays almost never achieve heights of more than 30 feet.

While a majority of visitors seek out the mountains of western Massachusetts to see this popular set of cascades, it's important not to be overtaken by tunnel vision and miss out on the rest of the scenery. An "endless variety of attractions" await those who do even the most minor of exploring of the area's eclectic environs.[118] Just be mindful of the rugged terrain while doing so. Along with being one of the most beautiful waterfalls of the Northeast, it's also one of the most deadly. Over twenty-five deaths have been recorded around Bash Bish during the last one hundred years. Let's not add another ghost to the already crowded bunch. Although, I could think of places much worse to spend eternity than near this divine waterfall.

The Legend of Bash Bish

Deemed guilty of adultery, a young woman by the name of Bash Bish was condemned to die by members of her tribe. The Mahicans viewed this act as an unpardonable crime, despite the allowance of polygamy and divorce in their society. Because she was well liked, and no one in her tribe could bear the thought of personally being responsible for causing her demise, it was determined to consign her fate to the forces of nature. Her unusual execution was to take place at the site of a large, rapidly flowing waterfall in the western Taconics. She was to be strapped into a canoe and sent to plunge over the falls, where she would undoubtedly be dashed to pieces on the sharp rocks below, afforded little protection from the thin-skinned birch bark canoe she was destined to ride in.

At sunrise on the day of execution, Bash Bish was tightly bound into the canoe and only moments away from being launched into the foaming brook, when a dense fog quickly swept down the narrow ravine, obscuring everything. Out of view, Bash Bish somehow managed to undo her restraints and free herself. Knowing that she could never return to her friends or family, and finding the idea of having to start anew elsewhere absolutely repugnant, she decided to accept the punishment of death. However, it was to be done on her terms.

Just as she clambered to the top of a massive boulder sitting at the edge of the precipice that divides the falls, the fog dissipated as quickly as it had arrived, and Bash Bish was once again in full public view. Everyone from her tribe was in attendance, gathered around the edge of the deep plunge pool at the base of the falls, including her infant daughter, White Swan.

As she stood atop the crag, silently gazing down at her people, a mass of butterflies, as numerous as the individuals congregated to watch her die, appeared seemingly from thin air and began to encircle her head like a crown. With every pass they picked up speed. What began as light fluttering quickly intensified into a frenzied swarm of activity. When the shocked onlookers half expected a tornado to erupt from the ceaseless and turbulent rotation, Bash Bish leapt off the cliff, with the butterflies following her into the mist of the raging cataract. Though a long and thorough search of the plunge pool took place, her body was never recovered. Because of the sudden fog, prolific and strange behavior of the butterflies, and her vanishing without a trace, people began to suspect that Bash Bish was a witch.

***

Despite her mother's tarnished reputation, White Swan managed to do quite well for herself. She had grown to become as lovely as her mother had been. Upon reaching adulthood, she married the son of the tribe's chief. For years they lived in nearly perfect contentment. As time wore on, however, things took a turn for the worse when it became obvious that White Swan would never be able to bear her husband any children. Needing an heir to carry on his family's legacy, he was forced to take an additional wife.

Overcome with sadness and needing an escape from the village, she began to take long walks into the wilderness. One day her aimless wandering brought her back to the fateful waterfall, a spot she hadn't visited since her days as an infant. Her relatives did all in their power to keep her away from the area, which, since the odd occurrences of her mother's botched execution, was regarded with an equal mixture of awe and apprehension.

That night as she lay in a deep sleep, her mind was overcome with a vivid dream of her mother beckoning for her to return to the site of the waterfall. In the morning she did as the dream commanded and visited the spot again. In her society, dreams were not to be dismissed; rather, they were thought to be divine revelations that were to be carefully analyzed and heeded.

Day after day, White Swan sat along a boulder at the brim of the falls, dangerously close to the swift current, awaiting another message from Bash Bish, as the dream foretold would come to her at this very spot. Her husband, worried about the depressed and fixated state of his wife—whom he still loved with all his heart—did everything in his power to improve her spirits. Each day as she hovered at the edge of the cliff, despondent and mindlessly staring into the churning water below, he would bring her a new gift from the forest, a small token of his affection.

On the tenth day, he came across a rare find. In a grove of cardinal flowers, a pure-white butterfly was alighted on one of the fiery blossoms. With the stealth that was natural to his race, he quickly crept up to the insect unnoticed and clutched it, imprisoning it in the hollow of his hands. Instantly, he set off to present his proud catch to White Swan. No sooner had he given the rare insect to her, she began to hear her mother's voice echoing from the plunge pool below. In a beautiful, intoxicating tone, Bash Bish urged her daughter to join her in the spirit world, where no worries or strife, she promised, could ever touch her. White Swan obeyed and stepping off the ledge, disappearing into the mist, the white butterfly trailing close behind. Her husband rushed to pull her back, but it was too late. In his eagerness to save her he had disregarded his own safety and, slipping on the slick, moss-covered rocks, tumbled down the falls. As happened with her mother before her, no trace of White Swan was ever found. Her husband's badly battered and broken body, however, was cast up from the emerald-tinted pool and washed ashore.

***

The area surrounding the falls is notoriously dangerous.

Visitors to the falls today, especially on drab, foggy days, occasionally report encounters with the supernatural. Smiling faces are said to be seen in the foam of the plunge pool, while alluring, siren-like voices sometimes whisper from the spray of the tumbling water. A number of the numerous deaths that have occurred in the vicinity over the years have been attributed to these ghostly manifestations. Some say that they're the mischievous workings of an evil witch; others, that they're derived from melancholy spirits who dwell beneath the water, eager to acquire new companions to assuage their own loneliness. Either way, this curious waterfall is one best approached with a healthy dose of caution.

Getting There

Two parking areas offer access to Bash Bish Falls; one is located in New York and the other in Massachusetts.

The New York lot is part of Taconic State Park in Copake Falls, NY 12517. From the intersection of Routes 22 and 344, follow Route 344 east for about 1.25 miles. The parking area is on the right (42.117112, -73.507736). To visit the falls, proceed along the wide and gently ascend blue-blazed Bash Bish Falls Trail for 0.75 miles.

To find the Massachusetts lot, continue east along Route 344 for another mile. The parking area will also be on the right (42.115049, -73.491568). At an elevation of around 1,250 feet, expansive views of the Harlem Valley can be taken in by walking to an overlook a short distance to the east. While the hike to the falls is shorter from this spot, it's substantially steeper and more rugged. Take the blue-blazed trail downhill for about a quarter of a mile.

17 Spook Rock

In the town of Greenport in central Columbia County, the Claverack Creek snakes its way across a flat to gently rolling pastoral setting, ultimately merging with another minor creek before entering the Hudson River. Parcels of cropland and pasture surround this tributary of the Hudson as far as the eye can see, studded here and there with historic farmhouses and family plots. It's a fine example of country living and a throwback to an earlier era when most of the region had the same rustic look. The land is so well suited for cultivation and continually exudes an unsurpassed tranquility that, like meat in a smokehouse, its contents have been well preserved. These same traits that captivate today made the area a prime dwelling site for native peoples millennia ago. It is, therefore, little surprise that "at one of the most picturesque spots in the creek," an old legend pertaining to the Indians continues to cast its spell among the minds of residents and visitors alike.[119]

At the eastern base of Becraft Mountain, where Claverack Creek all but touches the mountain's slopes, a large boulder known as Spook Rock sits partially submerged in the current. A multitude of boulders sprout from the center of the creek along this stretch of water, though Spook Rock far surpasses the size of the others. For those unaccustomed to this landmark, one need not try to determine which stone is the largest; a bright-crimson historical marker adjacent to a sizable pull-off along Spook Rock Road near the creek gives notice. It is indeed one of the most picturesque spots around.

The creek here is lined with overarching trees that cast a sun-dappled shade, which is greatly amplified in the afternoon hours by the verdant slopes of the looming Becraft Mountain just to the west. The water radiantly sparkles beside a lush herbaceous layer that graces the creek's slanted banks, containing tall, sweet-smelling grasses and a modest assortment of colorful wildflowers that are seen populating the meadows nearby in great numbers. On the downstream side of Spook Rock, the surface is

Jerusalem artichokes, a type of perennial sunflower, in bloom near Spook Rock in September.

dimpled by gentle backward-swirling eddies and is comparatively still, shielded from the rushing waters that surround. Here the creek is like glass, which, depending on the angle of the sun, is perfectly reflective and functions as a great mirror, but at other times, the sun melts through the liquid medium, making it fully transparent and giving an unimpeded glimpse of the creek's bottom and aquatic inhabitants.

These traits have made this a popular swimming hole in years past. Old postcards from the early 1900s show images of children perched atop Spook Rock, ready to jump in. It's still as alluring now as it was back in the day.

It's in the vicinity of Spook Rock that legend and fact merge. The land along the creek was heavily settled by Native Americans thousands of years ago and used as seasonal winter camps. Plows routinely unearth Indian relics in the area, among them arrowheads, grooved axes, and fragments of pottery, indicating not only an aboriginal presence but giving an idea as to their numbers and habitation dates. Certain artifacts can be rather precisely dated, especially when it comes to projectile points. The shape of the points evolved over time, so it is possible to give an approximate age. From artifacts recovered on Becraft Hill and on what is now farmland along Spook Rock Road, it appears that habitation stretches all the way back to the Early Archaic period (8000–6000 BCE). Fluted points recovered from nearby areas of Columbia County, however, indicate a Native American presence going back over 10,000 years. The Indians are reputed to have called a village of theirs in the Claverack area "Potcoke."

Directly across the road from Spook Rock, at the base of Becraft Mountain, and at a location slightly farther south, rock overhangs provided shelter to the

Perkiomen broad point (2000–500 BCE).

Indians. These rockshelters gave relief from the elements and, being made from stone, required no maintenance and so were very convenient. Beginning in the 1940s, archeologists excavated the rockshelters, recovering a wide variety of artifacts that showed the area was used as a seasonal settlement. Some objects in the caves were too large and unwieldy to constantly move from one area to another, such as fragile pottery vessels. If the rockshelters were used erratically for a night or two by passing Indians, only smaller artifacts such as projectile points, scrapers, and bones would likely have been recovered.

Based on the artifacts recovered, and what we know of the Indians by historical accounts, we can say the pleasant terrain around Claverack Creek was utilized primarily in the winter months. During the summer, regional Indians lived along the Hudson River, fishing and using the river for travel. But when colder weather arrived, they moved inland to hunt, as well as to escape the harsh winter winds. The lee created by Becraft Mountain would have significantly diminished the predominating westerly winds.

Due to the copious quantities of artifacts unearthed by local farmers, it is hardly surprising that a myth emerged tying a prominent, highly visible stone to that of the Indians. It's not difficult to envision a group of young swimmers frolicking in the deep holes around Spook Rock, imagining the same spot being similarly utilized centuries earlier by bands of "noble savages." In their reverie and fertile Romantic-era imaginations, it's easy to see local residents trying to preserve a bit of their memory by suffusing the boulder with legend. Spook Rock served as a headstone, as it were, to native culture.

The Origin of Spook Rock

Legend has it that countless years ago, long before the first white man stepped foot in what is now Columbia County, the chief of the Mahicans lived in a wigwam at the top of Becraft Mountain. His lofty dwelling was a defensive maneuver, the result of his tribe warring with numerous enemies.

The chief had a beautiful daughter "whose soft dark eyes and raven locks, and nut-brown skin were a bewitchment."[120] One day a warrior from an enemy tribe, searching for weaknesses in the Mahicans' defenses, climbed the mountain and, nearing the site of the chief's wigwam, spotted his peerless daughter gracefully sauntering through the wooded aisles. It was love at first sight.

What occurred next is murky—we know not how the enemy warrior approached her or what words he spoke, but his actions were successful, and the Indian princess became enamored. Thereafter the warrior would sneak back at night, and the two would rendezvous away from prying eyes near the Claverack Creek. These meetings continued for several months. Despite the two being from warring tribes, they were determined to be together, but like the tragic tale of Romeo and Juliet, they met with grave misfortune.

After an interval of some length, the girl worked up the courage to speak to her father about her suitor, but he instantly dismissed the notion of them ever being together. After this, the chief kept a watchful eye on his daughter, and it became nearly impossible to sneak away at night to meet her lover. It continued this way for weeks, but finally an opportunity arose. The Mahicans, successful in one of their campaigns against one of their several enemies, decided to hold a large religious celebration to give thanks for their victory. Amid the jubilation the princess expected to remove herself without anyone noticing. And so, with the aid of a trusted messenger, she sent word to the warrior that he should meet her at their usual rendezvous point the following evening.

And she was correct—in the heat of the celebration she found little difficulty in exiting the large congregation without being spotted. As soon as she was out of sight of the crowd, she dashed down the mountain and joined her lover at their usual meeting place along the creek. The main topic of discussion was elopement. They decided that they wanted to start their lives anew, far away from both their tribes. Just as they began discussing possible destinations, a rumble of thunder was heard in the distance, and within minutes the storm was upon them. Suddenly, a bolt of lightning struck a cliff behind the two, detaching a large fragment of rock that careened into the creek below, taking with it the secret lovers. The storm passed as quickly as it arrived, and the only trace left of the pair was a single moccasin clinging to the side of the stone near the waterline.

Another version of the story tells of the lovers meeting on a boulder in the creek, and that a massive flood swept them away to their doom.

In both versions, the storm, it is said, was brewed by Manitou, the Great Spirit, in punishment of the lovers' disobedience of their parents and for shirking the sacred ceremony held in his honor.

The moral of the story is that God is vigilant and watches at all times, even when human eyes are not. He will not hesitate to show his displeasure. This legend is perhaps more Christian than it is Indian. It's Old Testament justice masked behind an Indian facade. What better way to solidify the tenets of obedience and worship to wayward children than by incorporating them into a tale that showed that even "savage" culture embraced these beliefs. It sends a strong message by implying that those who ignore these tenets, even in the name of love, must be more uncivilized than even the heathen Indians.

The last part of the legend maintains that whenever the church bell in Claverack tolls, Spook Rock turns over and the lovers briefly reappear. It's a quaint tale for a quaint spot.

A note in an 1890s travel guide mentioned that the location "is visited on moonlight nights by the neighboring swains and their sweethearts, who linger to see it turn in its shiny bed when it hears the institute bell."[121] Low moans of the Indian princess are sometimes to be heard near the fateful boulder as the dismayed ghost searches for her lost love.

Spook Rock marks the site of a depressing narrative of young love literally crushed. Despite the warning the tale issues, the stone has served as a prominent rendezvous point for lovers over the years. To some, the idyllic, pastoral setting is simply romantic, and the tale heightens the ambiance; but to young lovers engaging in relationships not sanctioned by parents, a visit might just be tempting fate.

A historical marker next to an excellent fishing spot along Claverack Creek.

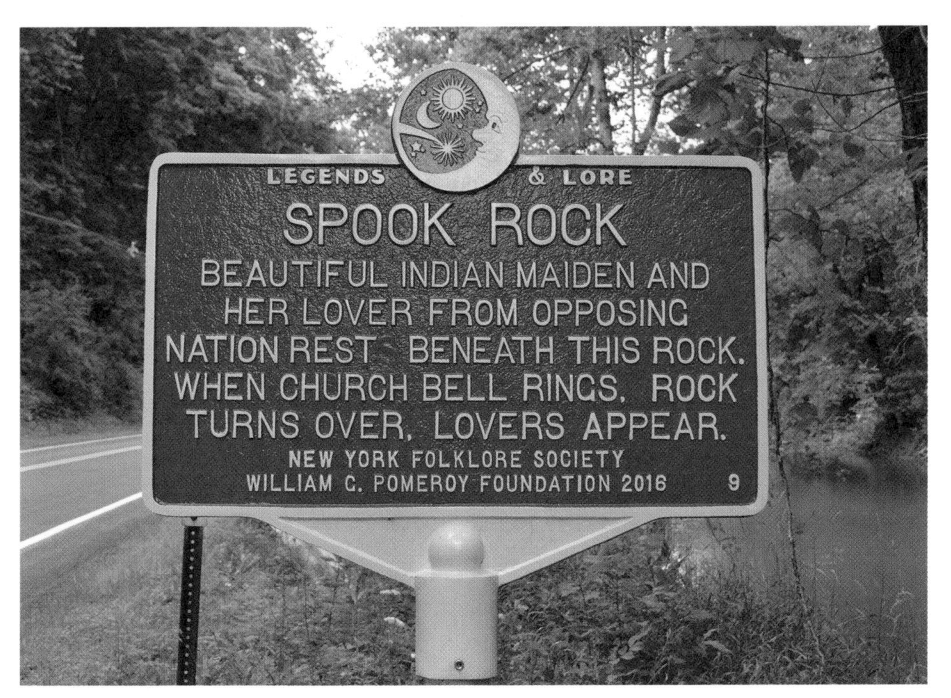

Getting There

Parking for Spook Rock is at a pull-off (42.224883, -73.757988) along the appropriately named Spook Rock Road in Hudson, NY 12534. It's 0.7 miles south of the road's intersection with Route 23B and 2.6 miles north of its intersection with Route 23. Spook Rock is about 100 feet north of a red historical marker at the pull-off.

13 Devil in the Catskills

The early settlers of southern New York found the Catskill Mountains as intimidating as they are tall and looming. These mountains are in stark contrast to what the settlers had first encountered as they made their way inland from the mostly flat environs of the Hudson River. The open forests of the charming Hudson Valley were easily felled and transitioned into fertile planting fields, whereas the rocky, dense, and hellish landscape of the Catskills thwarted even the staunchest of Christians, who felt it their duty to attempt to develop and cultivate every bit of wild land they encountered for the glory of God. Europeans saw this area as the playground of the Devil, and in their failing to successfully tame the land blamed the Evil One for their misfortune. If the Devil didn't hold sway of the region prior to colonization, he certainly does now, with his name plastered to countless landmarks, from natural stone features to popular hiking trails.

While farming in the Catskills, for the most part, was not practical, the region possessed two other main elements that made men saunter onward to risk their necks. The mountains contained vast stores of timber and were imbued with a sublime beauty, which only as time progressed would be adequately appreciated. While the lumber itself was valuable and sent to the mills for a tidy profit, the real prize was the bark of hemlock trees. Hemlock bark contains high levels of tannins, which are perfect for tanning, or curing leather. Hemlocks most often occur in damp areas of steep terrain, such as the sides of mountains and ravines. As such, they grew in profusion in the rugged Catskills. Tanneries were created in remote areas, and around them sprung up towns. As the more accessible mountain slopes began to be denuded, people began to take notice of the beauty they were losing. The Catskills later became a prime destination for artists, many of whom belonged to the burgeoning group of landscape painters now referred to as the Hudson River School. As time wore on and people admired the resulting artwork, tourism and the hospitality industry exploded, creating a whole new enterprise that drastically shifted the economic dynamic from resources to services, thus further helping the conservation of the Catskills.

Hell Hole Brook plunges into the Devil's Kitchen.

Early on, before the lumber industry emerged and painters arrived, the Catskills were trackless and nearly impenetrable. The first pioneers had a hard time negotiating their way through the mountains. Mainly, they created routes through steep stream valleys known in the region as "cloves" (another reference of the devil, on the basis of the belief that he has cloven hooves). Throughout the Catskills, conditions are often treacherous and have caused many an untimely demise. The land here is constantly shrouded in fog or clouds, and the risk of slipping is commonplace. Moreover, low branches often hide bottomless crevasses and beetling precipices. In short, these mountains are undeniably dangerous. Each year, people on a simple jaunt through the forest fail to make it home from misplaced footing and a bit of bad luck. In pioneer times it was likely more so. The region contained the perfect elements for the development of legends and ghost stories.

The howling wilderness that presented itself to these intrepid first explorers was beset with fearsome creatures. The Catskills are so named from the wild cats—namely, mountain lions—that once prowled the dark forests in abundance. While mountain lions and wolves have long since disappeared, venomous snakes and other predators are still present and, in some cases, quite prevalent in certain areas. Moreover, the mountains were used as hunting preserves by local Native American tribes. Only later did the area become more used for habitation as the natives were forced to take refuge here from hostile settlers. Native Americans also believed a good chunk of the Catskills to be under the spell of the supernatural. As a result, they tended to avoid the mountains, or at least certain areas they thought were inhabited by *Manitous*—demigods or powerful spirits. These beliefs may have helped bolster European notions that the mountains were under the dominion of Satan.

Devil's Kitchen

The Devil's Kitchen possesses some of the finest scenery in the Catskills. The area is a deep gorge in the upper reaches of Platte Clove that contains lofty cliffs, along with numerous waterfalls, cascades, and deep crystalline pools. Its approximate location is at the confluence of the Plattekill Creek and Hell Hole Brook. The name reportedly comes about from the roiling pools of foamy water at the base of the falls, which are reminiscent of large cauldrons set to a boil and fiercely stirred by invisible demonic hands. What's more, it's said that the boulders that litter the stream are the Devil's kitchenware.

The area is popular with rock and ice climbers. But the main draw to many is the pristine waterfalls; about eighteen line the creek that flows through Platte Clove. Among the finest and tallest is Lower Rainbow Falls, towering to about 100 feet. It's made even more spectacular by the fact that visitors almost always have it to themselves. Unlike many other large waterfalls in the Catskills, Lower Rainbow Falls—and the entire Devil's Kitchen—has no trail access. Its inaccessibility ensures the primeval ambiance of the place remains. While no marked, sanctioned trail exists, this isn't to say that traditional bushwhacking is the only way to access it. An informal, unblazed path runs horizontally along the southern slope of the ravine. Getting to the stream at the bottom is a much more difficult bushwhack that involves climbing down a narrow gully lined with a jumbled heap of basketball-size stones, many of which are precariously perched and may tumble down the mountain with the slightest tap. The descent is extremely treacherous. There are few other routes to the bottom that don't involve traditional rock climbing. The location is mostly walled in by cliffs or nearly vertical slopes, and those not taking the area seriously may meet their end here. Unexperienced bushwhackers looking for an impressive waterfall to visit have other options.

Those not wishing to venture off trail can visit Platte Clove Falls. Although not technically part of the Devil's Kitchen, it's a close match that's located just above the deep, treacherous gorge that contains the more rugged scenery. It's an easy, short hike via a blazed and well-maintained trail system.

Charles Lanman, a frequent visitor of Platte Clove, recorded this about the upper part of the gorge in 1844:

> Caverns, too, and chasms are there, dark, deep, chilly, and damp, where the toad, the lizard and snake, and strange families of insects, are perpetually multiplying and actually seeming to enjoy their loathsome lives; the Black Chasm, and the Gray Chasm, and the Devil's Chamber, with perpendicular walls of twice the height of a tall mast, and with a wainscoting of pines and hemlocks, that have braved a thousand years the battle and the breeze.[122]

Accidents and Murder

The notoriously dangerous terrain of the Devil's Kitchen has resulted in numerous deaths over the centuries. Nearly every year, a hiker or other visitor is killed or seriously injured while in the heart of the ravine or simply near its rim along Platte Clove Road. Aside from countless accidents, at least one murder victim's body has been removed from the Devil's Kitchen. In 1925, while hunting for ginseng, a father and son stumbled across a badly decomposed body. Articles of clothing and a wedding ring helped confirm that this was none other than Anna Kuespert, an elderly woman who had gone missing from Saugerties nearly a month earlier.

To get to where she was found, the 71-year-old Anna would have needed to undertake a steep ascent, followed by rough bushwhacking, which, even to experienced explorers, proves more than daunting. Detectives determined that there would have been no conceivable way for the frail woman to access the area on her own accord. From this, and the fact that she had recently changed her will—cutting at least one member of her family off from a sizable inheritance—it was strongly surmised that she had been murdered and her body dumped here, probably in an attempt to make it appear as if she had fallen to her death.

Lower Rainbow Falls in the rugged confines of Platte Clove.

Ghost Lights

Strange lights and sounds have been reported in and around the gorge. At a campsite high above the Devil's Kitchen, people have been awoken in the dead of night by odd rustlings and muddied, unintelligible voices in the surrounding woods. One party reported that after emerging from their tents upon hearing these strange sounds, they looked into the distance and saw a stationary orb of light in the path they had taken to get to the small campsite. Thinking it was someone in need of help, they called out, but no reply was returned. The orb then began moving on a completely level plane, which they said would have been impossible for a human traveler, on account of the uneven terrain, downed trees, and thick understory. Shortly after beginning to float away from the group, it was joined by another orb. The ghostly duo then stopped and remained stationary for a few moments before vanishing. Deciding that it was probably best to leave immediately, the group quickly packed up and proceeded to venture out of the woods. While making their exit, they were plagued by the unnerving sounds they had heard earlier, though this time greatly amplified. The bushes behind them feverishly rustled, but when a flashlight was shone on them, nothing was to be found. By the time the group had made it back to the road, they were practically running from the supernatural terror that was always just behind them, no matter their speed.

Some of the odd noises that echo up from Platte Clove are attributed to boulders tumbling down the steep slopes or ice shelving off cliffs or waterfalls. While some thunderous booms are undoubtedly a result of natural processes, the voices many report hearing are not so easily explained. Moreover, the lights are even more difficult to rationalize, given the nature of their movements and presence in inaccessible locations. Could these lights be the exceedingly rare phenomenon known as ball lightning? While some have reported seeing these lights during stormy weather, just as many have seen them during perfectly tranquil periods when there hasn't even been the most minor of breezes.

Some speculate that these are the ghosts of Native Americans or unlucky folks who have perished in the gorge. Others, that it may be something entirely different. Perhaps it is the Manitou of legend or even a will-o'-the-wisp like those of Europe. The latter are said to lure travelers to some unpleasant situation, such as a swamp, or some other unlucky place that could lead to their doom. Might these lights, like those of the Old World, be attempting to lure passersby to the edges of cliffs—or are they less sinister and just want to make their presence known, and aside from giving a good scare, have no ill will? These questions and others remain. All that is certain is that these ghost lights and disembodied voices haunt the Devil's Kitchen and unpredictably appear to those nearby at night.

Hidden Treasure

It is said that the Devil is the guardian of all ill-gotten wealth. If that turns out to be the case, then he might just be guarding something of tremendous value tucked away in the eastern Catskills. Legend has it that long-lost bootlegging loot worth millions of dollars lies hidden somewhere in the vicinity of Phoenicia. You see, on his deathbed, Dutch Schultz, one of the country's most infamous gangsters, supposedly revealed that he buried a vast portion of his fortune for safekeeping in the woods near or around the quaint town just mentioned.

Before we get to the treasure in more detail, we must delve into the life of Arthur Flegenheimer, a.k.a. "Dutch Schultz." Little is known of the man in the early days of his life, except that he was born in 1902 in New York City and had first been arrested at the age of 17 for breaking and entering. Numerous arrests followed. By the time Prohibition rolled around, Arthur, now "Dutch Schultz," found his calling in the illicit liquor trade, owning several speakeasies in New York. He prospered over the years and achieved an infamous reputation. He was renowned for being particularly cruel to his enemies. He is said to have hung people by their thumbs from meat hooks. When it came to those who stole from him, he would stick his gun in their mouths and, without the least bit of hesitation, pull the trigger. And in at least one instance, he cut a man's heart out.

His success in bootlegging and other crimes eventually landed him on the radar of the New York special prosecutor Thomas Dewey. With dogged determination, Dewey did all in his power to put the man behind bars. But when it came to Schultz's more serious crimes, he came up empty. Lacking the requisite evidence to put Schultz away for what could have been a life sentence, or worse, Dewey switched tactics and tried to nail Schultz for tax evasion in 1933. It had worked to bring down Al Capone, and so, it was hoped, Schultz would meet a similar fate.

Schultz went into hiding and was listed by J. Edgar Hoover as public enemy number one. Eventually, he was put on trial (after he turned himself in) but managed to escape being found guilty. It's believed that jury tampering and a public-relations blitzkrieg that enhanced his image in the public eye made his acquittal possible.

Right around the time of his indictment, Schultz and his bodyguard "Lulu" Rosenkrantz ventured upstate with a vast portion of the bootlegging fortune in tow and set about finding a hiding place for the loot. Schultz was worried that his luck was about to run out and that he would ultimately receive a prison sentence. He reasoned that if this were to happen, his money could be seized by the government, and upon being released from prison, he wouldn't have a dime to his name. Schultz was rightly worried. Many of his friends who had been imprisoned on similar charges had a hard time making a living after they had completed their time, not only because they had lost their money, but also because former territory had been claimed by rivals. In his estimation, burying his money was the best bet to ensure a comfortable retirement.

Many theories abound as to exactly how much the hidden trove is worth and exactly what it consists of. The only thing that's clear is that the treasure was placed in some type of steel trunk or metal suitcases. In terms of value, the figure that's most often quoted is from five to nine million dollars. Some say the cache is composed solely of cash or liberty bonds, others that it's a combination of gold coins, jewelry, and cash.

It's said that Schultz never returned to reclaim his wealth and that to this day it awaits discovery. In 1935, while at the Palace Chop House, a tavern in New Jersey that Schultz used as his headquarters while lying low, a rival gang ambushed the establishment and shot the entirety of Schultz's crew. Schultz received multiple bullet wounds but managed to initially survive the attack. He was rushed to the hospital and surrounded by police, who bombarded him with a series of questions. A stenographer recorded everything Schultz said up until the time of his death, which took place about twenty-four hours after the massacre. Much of what was recorded is little more than a jumble of incoherent ramblings, a result of a 106-degree fever that had caused him to become delirious. But there were moments of lucidity. Several statements he made provided the initial indication to the world that he had secreted money somewhere. Later, testimony of several of his supposed acquaintances bolstered that notion.

The author stands beside the "Devil's Tombstone."

A majority of opinions place the location of the treasure in Phoenicia between the railroad tracks and the Esopus Creek, which the railroad runs along. Rumor has it that Schultz and Rosenkrantz buried it at the base of a poplar tree that they had marked with an "X" in privately owned woods, unbeknownst to the owner.

The other group of believers thinks that the cache is located just outside Phoenicia along Route 214, somewhere near the Devil's Face or Devil's Tombstone, two prominent rocky landmarks within Stony Clove Notch. The Devil's Face is on a cliff high above the road, but the Devil's Tombstone is located just off the shoulder. The latter landmark is much easier to access. Most believe Schultz's deathbed riddle of "don't let Satan draw you too fast" pertains to the Devil's Tombstone, a hefty, upright natural slab of stone resembling a tremendous grave marker.[123] With Schultz and Rosenkrantz both being city folk, it's reasoned, they likely wouldn't have headed deep into the woods on steep terrain to bury the treasure and thus deposited it instead somewhere near the much more accessible Devil's Tombstone. Much digging has been done in all the areas mentioned over the years, but none has unearthed a single clue to the treasure's whereabouts or even whether it actually exists. Aside from the shaky ramblings of a delirious man and suspect statements from people who are said to have known Schultz, there is little concrete evidence to back up the claims of the treasure's existence.

Still, to this day, several people venture forth into the wilds of the eastern Catskills each year in search of Dutch Schultz's lost millions. If it does exist, the treasure might just be under the protection of the Devil and not likely to be discovered until a bargain is struck.

According to superstition, St. John's Eve (June 23) might be the most propitious time to undertake a search. It is said that hidden treasures are more easily revealed on this day than any other and may emit a glow indicating their whereabouts. And for those looking to make a deal, "St. John's Eve is the only evening in the year when his Satanic Majesty reveals himself in his proper shape to the eyes of men."[124]

Whether hunting for treasure or sublime scenery, the Catskills will provide you with something to remember. Be it the Devil's Kitchen or the Devil's Path, a 25-mile-long trail that traverses the most-rugged mountains of the region and ascends and descends a total of 14,000 feet, the landscape beckons and deceives. As I remember it:

The waterfalls and endless viewpoints are like sirens calling you to your doom. You rush, clamber down treacherous slopes without minding your step—and with misplaced footing on a slanted, dewy, lichen covered rock, you go airborne. Your eyes, now gazing skyward, catch blurry glimpses of overarching trees mingled with the smallest traces of blue, before going dark in an instant as you crash down upon the same uneven, slick piece of red sandstone, and you find yourself on your back with intense pain radiating all over. You rush to gauge the extent of your injuries, thinking the worst. Whew!—nothing broken—just some bruises and a stiff arm from trying to catch yourself. You take a moment of composure and then proceed again on your way, promising to be more careful. This promise is ludicrously short lived. When the next wonder presents itself, the siren's call begins once more, and under hypnotic spell you bathe in a sea of forgetfulness. Again, the cycle repeats. What will this next fall have in store? And in rhythmic fashion, things continue the same until you're either too battered to move or you've had your fill for the day. It's Russian roulette, really. But to adventurous spirits it might just be worth the while to tempt fate—or the Devil—to bask in the magnificent scenery and unrivaled splendor of the hidden recesses of the Catskill Mountains.

Getting There

The parking area for the Devil's Kitchen is located at 2425 Platte Clove Road, Elka Park, NY 12427. It's important to keep in mind that the steep, windy section of Platte Clove Road just east of the parking area is closed from November to May. Those venturing to the locale from the Hudson Valley during the offseason must take a lengthy detour through Palenville, following Route 23A westward.

The Devil's Kitchen is a broad area with loose boundaries, but its traditional northern fringe can be seen by walking a few hundred feet east along Platte Clove Road from the parking area. The Hell Hole Brook flows under a stone bridge and into a treacherous gorge (Devil's Kitchen). While there are many ways to access the bottom of the gorge, the vast majority are too dangerous to undertake without rock-climbing equipment.

One of the safer routes is to follow Plattekill Creek down the mountain from Plattekill Falls. From the parking area, walk west along the shoulder of the road for about a quarter mile until you reach the Catskill Center's Platte Clove Preserve on the left. Take the yellow-blazed Waterfall Trail for a third of a mile. Once at the falls, go to the south side of the creek and follow it as it flows down the mountain. Within a few hundred feet, an informal, unmarked footpath will emerge. Follow this for about 0.2 miles. The trail will essentially disappear when a conspicuous rocky gully emerges on your left. Carefully climb down it to reach the bottom of Platte Clove. Assuming you went the right way, this route will bring you to the base of Lower Rainbow Falls (42.130764, -74.082464). Welcome to the Devil's Kitchen / Platte Clove. Another 15–20 waterfalls and cascades can be found farther downstream; none are as large as Lower Rainbow Falls. Platte Clove extends for miles beyond this point, most of which is part of the Catskill Forest Preserve.

*** **This is the most dangerous hike listed in this book.** There's a serious chance of injury descending to the bottom of Platte Clove. Rocks are slick and are not always stable, not to mention the numerous cliffs and steep slopes that abound here. Take adequate precautions if you decide to undertake the journey.

Devil's Tombstone

From the intersection of Routes 23A and 214 in the town of Tannersville, NY 12485, take Route 214 southwest for 3.2 miles. The Devil's Tombstone (42.155002, -74.205491) will appear on the left, located at the end of a small parking area less than 100 feet from the road. The surrounding campground is named after the diabolical monolith.

Kaaterskill Falls

Kaaterskill Falls begins its life at the top of a deep and narrow ravine that's a spur of the larger Kaaterskill Clove, which Route 23A steeply follows as it snakes its way between the towns of Palenville and Haines Falls. Standing at 260 feet high, this is the tallest waterfall in New York State; that is, if we happen to overlook the fact that the waterfall is double tiered and doesn't fall uninterruptedly for the full distance. After plunging straight down for 180 feet, the water crashes onto a broad, flat terrace. The pummeling of the stone over the centuries has created a deep, circular plunge pool in the center. From an outlet in this basin, the water cascades an additional 80 feet from another sheer cliff and then continues to madly dash down the mountain in the confines of a primeval stream, overhung with dark hemlocks and birches and dotted with a wide spread of colorful wildflowers. Several other smaller waterfalls can be found along the stream's course before the tumbled, fomented water eventually, after some distance, ends its frenzied journey in the still and placid waters of the Hudson, far below its initial dive off the rugged mountainside.

The sublimity and grandeur of the waterfall and its surroundings attracted numerous Romantic writers and painters of the nineteenth century, hoping to capture the beauty of the scene through their artistic medium of choice or gain inspiration from it, using it as a sort of muse. They viewed the Catskills, and especially this spot, as a sanctified landscape. Washington Irving, William Cullen Bryant, Henry David Thoreau, Thomas Cole, and Sanford Gifford are only a few prominent writers and artists to pay the site a visit. Kaaterskill Falls even attracted President Chester Arthur in August 1884. Aside from these distinguished individuals, the falls drew countless tourists also wanting to imbibe the potent scenery. They came in flocks for a variety of reasons. Some believed that the crisp mountain air would improve their bodily health, while others sought out the place to have a spiritual communion with nature. And then there were those who came mainly for amusement, vacationing in the mountains to gawk at a unique spectacle while taking leave from hectic city life.

Kaaterskill Falls is 260 feet tall.

The beauty of the scenery was undeniable. Even if the mountain air failed to act as a panacea, it worked to uplift the spirits, at least. Almost no one went away disappointed, at least initially, before development of the area increased. Benson Lossing, an early Hudson Valley historian and sketch artist, believed Kaaterskill Falls to be "one of the wildest and most romantic rambles in the world."[125] The significant height of the falls, especially the first cascade, always made for an impressive show. In 1893, one visitor observed, "In front, the falls, twisted hither and thither by the winds, assume fantastic and distorted shapes, twinkling and glistening in the sunlight like a veil of diamonds."[126] The scene was compounded, too, in winter, when vast ice columns and icicles would emerge. Thomas Cole, a Hudson River School painter who put Kaaterskill Falls on the map with his iconic depiction of the scene, remarked that the frozen appendages "look like gorgeous chandeliers, or the richest pendants of a Gothic cathedral—wrought in crystal."[127] "We left the spot," Cole says, "with lingering steps and real regret."[128]

By the start of the twentieth century, this part of the Catskills had seen such a surge of popularity that several large-scale hotels had been strategically constructed nearby to accommodate the influx of visitors. These "mountain houses" commercialized, and often degraded, the landscape. The Laurel House, situated precariously close to the edge of Kaaterskill Falls, destroyed the sense of isolation by bringing aspects of the city to the mountains. Apart from the structure intruding on the wild character of the area when it was seen looming at the top of the cliff next to the waterfall from below, the main floor of the building contained a curio shop that sold trinkets and other souvenirs, eroding the spiritual significance of the area. Moreover, the greedy owners turned the once-powerful, free-flowing falls into a weak and cheapened spectacle. And by cheapened, I mean a downgraded display; a view of the falls wasn't exactly cheap, since an admission fee was charged to see this natural wonder—and not to just gain entry. A dam was constructed a short distance upstream of the falls that all but eliminated water flow to the once-untamed cataract during hot and dry summer months. The desiccated falls could be revived for a fee of twenty-five cents. After paying, a worker would open the dam's spillway, thus unleashing the collected water, and the falls would temporarily be reborn. Many complained of the "certain pecuniary trickeries connected with [Kaaterskill Falls'] grim majesty."[129]

Washington Irving did his part to attract people to Catskill Mountains when he penned the short story "Rip Van Winkle" in 1819. Aside from the dramatic imagery he conjures up of the Catskills, the legend he created was immensely popular, and whenever someone thought about these mountains, they equated it with the tale of the eponymous main character of Irving's story. There was something profoundly charming in the misfortune—or serendipity, depending your take on it—of Rip being hoodwinked by a group of nine-pin-playing gnomes into taking a draught of magic liquor that resulted in putting the poor man to sleep for twenty years.

All those who came to stay at the mountain houses bombarded the employees with questions pertaining to the iconic tale. There was a virtual obsession of wanting to know exactly where Rip Van Winkle slept. Though Irving never explicitly states in the story where the meeting with the gnomes took place, his description of the area sounds a lot like what is seen around the vicinity of Kaaterskill Falls. A newspaper article from 1889 states: "There are people living who claim that Irving himself, in describing his ride from Catskill up the Kaaterskill Clove, admitted that this was the place he had in view when he presented Rip Van Winkle to the world."[130]

When a hotel owner was asked how tired he was of answering questions pertaining to the story of Rip, he replied, "It pleases people to hear it, and I like to please them; it pays."[131] And it certainly did pay to cater to people's love of the affable Rip Van Winkle. The story made the mountains more attractive and magical and helped usher in new guests.

By 1920, visitation to the Catskills had drastically declined. The Adirondacks in northern New York, now more accessible through the increase of roads, railroads, and other advances, became the new outdoor playground of the state. The West had also opened up, and much tourist activity was lost to sites such as the Grand Canyon, Yellowstone, and the Rocky Mountains.

In newspapers and other advertisements, hotel owners extolled the health benefits of visiting the Catskills. They claimed that the area was mosquito free and therefore lacked malaria, and that the thin, clean mountain air assuaged the symptoms of tuberculosis (a major epidemic of the time) and helped with problems relating to hay fever, asthma, loss of appetite, etc. They also frequently mentioned that their hotels were situated in a location that was always 15–20 degrees cooler than such places as New York City and parts of Pennsylvania. Many doctors of the time who were unable to successfully treat their patients suggested a change of scenery and often advocated the importance of visiting elevated locales. The higher Adirondacks and Rocky Mountains provided even cooler and fresher air than the Catskills. Moreover, western sites offered a substantially more significant change of scenery to easterners. Unable to adequately compete, the Catskill mountain houses were ultimately forced to close their doors as visitation gradually waned.

Today, Kaaterskill Falls and much of the land once occupied by the hotels are part of the Catskill Forest Preserve. Only remnants of the structures remain, most having burned down long ago, either accidentally or having been set on fire purposely by New York State to rid the land of the decrepit buildings.

Genesis

A geologist will tell you the mighty Kaaterskill Falls is approximately 15,000 years old, a product of the last Ice Age. While the ravine that the falls flow through is partly the result of glacial scouring, much of it was shaped by the tremendous meltwaters that raged down the mountain as the weather warmed and the Laurentide ice sheet began to shrink and retreat northward. What we see flowing through the ravine today is but a trickle compared to the monstrous deluge that formerly tore deeply into the rock, creating the steeply sloped topography. Since the melting first began, the waterfall, like the glacier, has retreated upstream, as the rock underneath the falls gradually eroded. Kaaterskill Falls has moved north slightly less than a mile since the start of things. While movement upstream continues to occur today, it does so at a snail's pace now that the water flow is greatly diminished from that of Ice Age days.

The unique two-tiered structure of the falls is the result of differing rock hardness. At the very top of Kaaterskill Falls is a cap of overlying sandstone that projects over the edge of the precipice like a lip. Sandstone is more resistant than the underlying shale and thus erodes slower. The rock of the Catskills is all sedimentary in origin, meaning the rock is stratified in distinct layers. Much of what is now the Catskills was once a series of shallow, marshy deltas created from the erosion of the ancient Acadian Mountains during the Devonian period (380–360 million years ago) Over

It's possible to walk behind the upper falls with a little careful negotiating of the slick terrain.

the eons as these peaks were slowly worn down, and rivers and other landscape features shifted, the deposited sediment changed in composition. At the bottom of the first cascade, the red shale has been deeply eroded back by the heavy spray and resulting freeze-thaw cycle in winter, creating the semicircular amphitheater that allows visitors to walk far behind the falls. The top of the second tier is composed of another layer of tough sandstone.

The Indians of the region had their own beliefs when it came to the creation of the falls. Thomas Longstreth, an early twentieth-century author who retold one of their tales regarding its birth, stated that "the geology book must not be trusted too implicitly."[132] To the native peoples, Kaaterskill Falls was not created slowly, the byproduct of glacial melting, but rather instantaneously by supernatural forces.

Most of the Catskills were looked upon as sacred ground and the abode of numerous spirits and deities. Useless for agriculture and too wild to meaningfully inhabit when the fecund Hudson Valley next door provided extraordinarily well, the Indians, for the most part, left the area alone, except occasionally using it as a hunting ground. The area around where the falls now stand was especially revered and considered the dwelling place of a powerful and mischievous deity, though some said it was none other than the Great Spirit, Manitou. Hunters venturing into the mountains made sure to avoid the place out of respect and fear. Those who ventured into the confines of the steep mountain defile generally met with misfortune. The deity often amused himself with taking the form of various animals and leading hunters who followed to the very edges of towering cliffs and raging streams before suddenly vanishing.

Legend has it that one day a hunter lost his way and penetrated the deity's sanctum. Eventually, as the hunter wandered, he came to the edge of a small lake. Beside its shore stood a massive, mossy boulder decorated with a spread of the finest and most-beautiful wildflowers the hunter had ever seen. Rising up from one edge of the boulder was a gnarled hornbeam tree. Amid its crooked branches were several gourd containers. The hunter dislodged one and saw that it contained a liquid, which the quite exhausted and thirsty man decided to taste. He found it to be excellent spring water and took the gourd with him as he continued his journey. Moments later, just as he began to ascend a rocky slope, he tripped and dropped the gourd. Upon hitting the ground, the container split open and unleashed a torrent of water that swept down the mountain valley, carrying the hunter along. The raging stream eventually came to the edge of a massive cliff, and, upon plunging down, Kaaterskill Falls was born. The unlucky hunter was swept over the edge and met his doom on the rocks below. The stream, which sprang from where the gourd was dropped, has been flowing ever since.

Another creation myth revolves around a white maiden who appeared among the Mohawks, who lived to the west of the Catskills. The maiden had "flaxen hair and blue eyes" and was a great curiosity to the Indians.[133] Pure-white animals were considered rare and holy, and the Mohawks regarded this sudden visitor more so, believing her to be the daughter of Manitou. Once a year they brought the maiden to live among the most sacred spot in the Catskills—the abode of Manitou—for a week, so she could receive her father's wisdom and instructions. It is not known whether she encountered Manitou or not, but she was certainly always very lonely during her stay, usually crying as the Indians dropped her off and departed. One year, the maiden was visited by a River Indian who came across her as he was hunting in the mountains. Almost immediately, the two struck it off, and the hunter kept the lonely girl company for the week. When her stay was almost up, he promised to return the following year.

For several years, these week-long trysts took place amid the scenic mountains, and each time the two fell deeper in love. Eventually, it came to the point where the hunter couldn't stand to be without his love for a majority of the year, and he asked the maiden to come live with him. She happily accepted the offer. Before the two were set to leave, the hunter decided to gather his beloved a handful of frail harebells growing on a perilous ledge.

While the two were conversing on how to start a life together, the Mohawks, trudging up the mountain to retrieve the maiden, spotted the pair together and became enraged by the presence of the River Indian who dared intrude on so scared a spot. As the hunter was engaged in his task of collection, the Mohawks approached the maiden. Sensing the fury of the Mohawks and their intention to harm her lover, she fled from them, racing downhill. They immediately followed. As she neared the brink of a precipice, she came to a halt; just when the Mohawks were about to seize her, she moved

Roseshell azalea blooms in profusion near the falls in late May to early June.

forward and leapt off the edge. During her descent, her snow-white garments and flaxen hair fluttered madly in the breeze and transformed into a stream of sparkling water and she disappeared among the heavy mist. Manitou, it seems, caught his daughter in his arms, and since that day the mighty cascade known as Kaaterskill Falls has been raging over the cliff. It is a testament of the power of the Great Spirit, as well as a reminder of how many tears are shed when true love is crushed.

"By the witching light of a midsummer moon," it has been reported, "the silvery white garments [of the maiden] seem to gleam through the waters of Kaaterskill, and the face will almost shape itself, then fade away."[134]

A more recent legend relating to the falls deals with a ghost dog, who, on each anniversary of his death, comes back to haunt the spot of his demise. In June 1868, a man and his spaniel "Vite" visited the falls. At the top of the first cascade, the man left Vite alone while he hiked down to the base of the falls to get a better look. As he approached the plunge pool on the second tier, Vite spotted his owner below and, in a misguided attempt to join him, jumped off the 180-foot cliff. An epitaph carved into the stone at the top of the falls memorializes the sad event.

A *New York Times* article from 1901 describes the haunting:

> They tell how toward midnight on every June 19 the ghost of the spaniel haunts the vicinity of the falls, and how, as the hands of the clock mark the witching hour, a succession of short, sharp barks is heard, followed by the flight of the apparition through the air over the falls into the precipice, whence arises a prolonged howl which echoes and reechoes.[135]

Few other ghosts are reported to haunt the area, which is a bit surprising, considering how many deaths have taken place at Kaaterskill Falls. During the past two centuries over 200 fatal accidents have occurred in the vicinity. As the spot has gotten more popular over the years, the numbers of deaths have increased dramatically. In 2014, the Department of Environmental Conservation decided to do something about the problem and began implementing new safety features. Despite the improvements, yearly deaths and serious injuries still take place.

Is it solely the rugged nature of the area that's causing the unfortunate accidents—or might the deity said to reside in the ravine still be punishing those who intrude? Best watch your step.

Since its discovery by the white man, Kaaterskill Falls has constantly been changing. As we have seen, the mountain houses have come and gone. So, too, have the falls' numerous names. Before "Kaaterskill" was established by the owner of the Hotel Kaaterskill, the waterfall was variously referred to as "Catterskill" and "Cauterskill," among other permutations. What's more, the falls were once even grander than they are now. During a rambunctious Independence Day celebration in 1820, a 50-ton boulder, perched and slightly overhanging the cliff at the top of the first cascade, was dislodged and sent careening down toward the plunge pool, where it smashed into countless pieces. No painting or sketch of the scene prior to the vandalism exists, but written reports make it sound as if it was the falls' pièce de résistance. While change is natural in the course of the life of a waterfall, as rocks shift and crumble under the power of the stream, we must be careful not to hasten it. I don't think Manitou would approve of the defacement and disrespect of one of his most cherished creations.

Getting There

There are two popular parking areas to access the trail system that leads to Kaaterskill Falls. The lower lot is directly along Route 23A in Haines Falls, NY 12436 (42.189922, -74.074180). From the fork in the road where Routes 23A and 32A meet in Palenville, take Route 23A west for 3.6 miles. The parking area is on the left and can hold thirty cars. It fills up extremely quickly on weekends. From the parking area, walk downhill along the shoulder of Route 23A for a little less than a quarter mile. Immediately after crossing the bridge that spans Spruce Creek, turn left onto the yellow-blazed trail. In about half a mile the base of the falls will be reached.

A larger parking area that is frequently used when the Route 23A lot is full is located at the very end of Laurel House Road in Haines Falls. Take the yellow trail to reach a platform that overlooks the falls. A short distance from the trailhead, the yellow trail splits. If you're looking to get to the base of Kaaterskill Falls, take the blue trail downhill.

Echo Lake & Overlook Mountain

Washington Irving, on his many trips sailing up and down the Hudson River as part of family visits to Albany, would, with watchful eye, fixate on the Catskill Mountains each time his sloop rode by the towering peaks. During tranquil periods "they are clothed in blue and purple, and print their bold outlines on the clear evening sky," he wrote, "but sometimes, when the rest of the landscape is cloudless, they will gather a hood of gray vapors about their summits, which, in the last rays of the setting sun, will glow and light up like a crown of glory."[136] Overlook Mountain is one peak in the great phalanx of mountains that border the Hudson that would have boldly displayed itself to Irving and undoubtedly set the gears in motion for creation of one of his greatest characters: Rip Van Winkle. This majestic rounded hill of immense height hides a realm of the fantastic and does more than just inspire from a distance. Overlook Mountain and its wild environs are said to now harbor, or at one time in the past to have harbored, spirits, mythical creatures, and real animals of cornucopic abundance.

Perhaps the most charming feature of Overlook Mountain is the idyllic lake that rests in the bosom of the mountain's northern slope about 1,000 feet below its 3,140-foot summit. This small, almost perfectly circular 12.8-acre body of water is one of only two natural lakes to occur in sections of the Catskill Park designated as true wilderness. Echo Lake, also variously referred to as Shue's or Shew's Lake in the past, from its eighteenth-century discoverer/owner Tunis Shew, is a popular destination with fishermen and backpackers. A lean-to and several campsites fringe the lake.

Its current name, Echo Lake, derives from the area's special qualities of reverberation. Yell or shout at the top of your lungs at the water's edge, and you're said to hear a sharp response issuing back from the neighboring cliffs surrounding the lake.

According to a nineteenth-century writer for the *New York Times*, the "echo" may have a little bite to it. In 1874, a small party of men and women ventured out to the lake and, once there, decided to test its echoing capabilities.

> One of the male members of the party had a rich, sonorous voice, and so he took upon himself the responsibility of waking up the slumbering echo. "Helloa!" rung out full and clear over the still water, but no response. Somewhat vexed, he once more repeated in a louder tone, "Helloa!" Then came an answer, sure enough, across the rocky bluff, "Shut up, you idiot, or I'll send a charge of shot in you." Without a word the party left for the hotel, and never again tried the virtue of this echo.[137]

During my first visit to Echo Lake, I had a similar experience, though decidedly less curmudgeonly. Stepping out onto a small boulder that projected out into the lake, I, too, shouted "Hello" as loud as possible. A few seconds later a clear and perfect mimic bounced back. I was startled as to how crisp and booming the echo was, and now thought that this place must indeed have one of the best echoes in the world! Again, I rang out "Hello." But this time around I got a mediocre response at best—I could barely make out my utterance. Perplexed, I tested it once more. This time around another clear "Hello" issued back, but the voice did not sound like mine. My curiosity now aroused, I peered to the opposite shore, and there, at the base of a rocky slope obscured by spindly trees and a few bushes, stood the faint profile of a man with a fishing pole in hand. Here was my "echo." Duped and a tad embarrassed, I ended my experiment and called it a day and headed back up the mountain.

So, regarding the echo of Echo Lake—there is indeed one to be found along the lake's shores, although it's likely to be far less pronounced than what's typically envisioned. Unless, of course, there's someone hiding on the other side trying to have a bit of fun with you.

Overlook Menagerie

Echo Lake contains many swampy sections along its periphery and is said to be filling in at a relatively rapid pace. But its shallowness and inky-black waters belie a hidden wealth—trout. Like many streams, rivers, and lakes of the pristine Catskills, this spot contains robust quantities of brook trout, some of which have reportedly weighed in at over 5 pounds (a true monster for the species).

The landscape painter and author Charles Lanman visited Echo lake around 1840. Venturing out with an experienced guide and a couple of friends, the company enjoyed an overnight stay at the lake and tried their hand at fishing. In a period of less than twelve hours, the company had managed to catch 102 trout.

Around the campfire, the 27-year-old guide, Peter Hummel, told many tales concerning his exploits around Echo Lake over the years to Lanman and his companions. The uneducated Hummel, who never attended a day of school in his life, was a bark gatherer by trade (hemlock bark was once used to tan leather) and, when not trying to make a living, took to the woods again in pursuit of adventure. In addition to the wealth of the water, Hummel told the men that the surrounding forests teemed with animal life and that he had spent many a pleasant day engaging in "harmless murders." Lanman recorded the guide's boasts: "In one day, he shot three deer; at another time,

Echo Lake.

a dozen turkeys; at another, twenty ducks; one night, an old bear; and again, half a dozen coons; and, on one occasion, annihilated a den of thirty-seven rattlesnakes."[138]

Regarding the latter creature, Overlook Mountain has long been known to possess great numbers of timber rattlesnakes. Around 1823, a particularly large snake was killed near Echo lake that "measured between five and six feet."[139] To this day, visitors of the area must keep a wary eye out for the venomous reptiles. I myself had a recent encounter with one not far from the water's edge while following a path that loops around the lake. Near the lake's southern tip, high grasses routinely obscure parts of the trail. It was here that a snake began to feverishly vibrate its tail at me as I approached while mindlessly ambling down the trail. Not until I heard its unmistakable rattle did I see the very large creature laid out in the center of the trail, hidden among the tousled grass. Luckily, it decided to issue a warning. If it hadn't, I might have stepped on the poor reptile, which could have been a fatal mistake for us both. Far too often, even when approached, these creatures fail to sound their characteristic warning. I consider myself extremely fortunate this one made its presence known loud and clear.

Vampires

In addition to the creatures mentioned, A. E. P. Searing in her book *The Land of Rip Van Winkle* records a legend concerning vampire-like beasts that once prowled the shores of Echo Lake and its surroundings.

According to Searing, long ago, when the Six Nations were at the height of their power, a brave Indian warrior named Haidoni used to regularly make the trek up Overlook Mountain to hone his prowess with the bow. At night, he would often cast his birchbark canoe into the placid waters of Echo Lake and drift aimlessly while scanning the shores for prey. Once upon the water, he would ignite gigantic pine knots and set them at the bow of the canoe and conceal himself behind sprays of hemlock branches. Deer and other curious creatures, attracted by the light, like moths to a flame, would sneak down to the water's edge to get a better look. Seeing the glare of their eyes, Haidoni would cast aside his covering, pull back his bowstring, and "thud!"—in an instant, whatever unlucky creature was in his sights had received a mortal wound. In this way, Haidoni would often dispatch as many deer as fingers on his hands in a single evening.

One night, as he lay in his canoe he could not help but be overcome by a powerful melancholy. The night was still and contained not a trace of the usual nightly sounds—the hooting of owls, the fluttering of bats, the treble of crickets, and the chatter or movements of squirrels and mice were all conspicuously absent. Profound, eerie, and foreboding silence enveloped the mountain.

Since launching himself upon the black waters of the lake many hours ago, he hadn't picked up his bow once. More time elapsed after his initial plunge into melancholy. Eventually, just as he was about to give up for the night, he saw "great glaring eyes of fire" emerge from the inky black of the forest.[140] In usual fashion, he raised his bow and launched his steadfast arrow. Upon hitting its mark, the most awful, unearthly scream rang out, echoing far and near across the lake and forest. Haidoni was so taken aback by this strange, bloodcurdling death howl that he immediately came to shore and, without looking to identify the source of it, quickly proceeded to a cave he often slept in once his nightly hunts had concluded.

While making his way up the mountain, his throat became parched and he decided to make a brief stop at a nearby spring to appease his growing thirst. As he stooped down to drink at a pool of clear water amid a cluster of small rocks, a hand emerged from a hollow log he was positioned against and clutched his leg. From the log emerged a young woman. Shaking with fear, she quickly told Haidoni her story of tribulation.

While on a hunting expedition amid the mountains with her tribe, she and her sister became separated from the main group. The two of them wandered for many days among the wild Catskills. "This Overlook Mountain," she said, "was infested with vampires, who nightly pursued them to suck their blood."[141] This very night as the two women slumbered, one of the ghouls located them. As the Indian maiden recounted, she was awoken in the middle of the night by the sounds of someone eating. Turning over, she witnessed a horrific sight! Her sister lay dead, and crouched over the body was a vampire that was gluttonously drinking the blood and consuming the flesh. The maiden fled and the vampire followed. After running no great distance, she managed to conceal herself in the hollow log. And as the beast rushed by without detecting her, she heard it scamper down to the vicinity of the lake.

Now knowing what unleashed the awful cry, Haidoni informed the maiden that the creature was dead. He took the woman under his protection and immediately set out for his village. The duo encountered several more of the bloodsuckers during the course of the night, but none were able to overcome Haidoni's arrows. It is said that for his bravery during battles past, the Great Spirit looked down upon Haidoni with great favor and made sure every arrow dealt a lethal blow. The two were shortly thereafter married, and it is rumored that their descendants returned to Overlook Mountain year after year to rid the area of the formidable vampires.

But now that the hunters are no more, have the vampires, like the rattlesnakes that slither in abundance among the clefts and boulders of Overlook today, made a rebound?

***

Another Indian legend pertains to Echo Lake. The story goes that the daughter of an Indian chief would secretly rendezvous with her lover here during the evening hours. Her father, unapproving of the match, had the young man killed. In response, the maiden tossed herself off a cliff that rises above the lake. Her spirit is said to haunt the area and appears regularly around midnight.

***

Visitors to Echo Lake have all this to mull over—trout, rattlesnakes, vicious bloodsuckers, and spirits. And in a sense, this is what makes this small body of water so appealing. It's recreation mixed with a healthy dose of trepidation. This is what the Catskill

Mountains are all about. It's not a quaint, worry-free vacation. For that, you could go to the beach or some pastoral setting where the sun illuminates all nooks and crannies, and everything is as it seems. But the primeval Catskills deliver something more—a raw sublimity that makes you feel as if you're a part of something and not merely a spectator. Here, you can catch your own food and fend off ghouls and creatures of real flesh and blood—taking your life into your own hands—all the while imbibing the fresh air and getting a bit of exercise.

These things are what made the mountain houses of the Catskills so popular. Guests of the Overlook Mountain House, only a short distance from the mountain's summit, would often make the descent from the hotel and take rowboats out onto the lake, and so it became a popular destination of day-trippers. While the boats are long gone, other remnants of the mountain's storied past continue to linger.

Once such lingering reminder is the ghostly remains of the Overlook Mountain House. Sizeable portions of the exterior remain standing and loom over the passersby who follow the carriage road turned trail to the summit of the mountain. What stands today is the third incarnation of the hotel. Its predecessors had the unfortunate luck of burning to the ground.

A Hotel Fit for a President

The first Overlook Mountain House opened its doors in 1871. A newspaper advertisement at the time described it as being a three-story structure with a French roof that contained 140 rooms. The long, broad piazza toward the entrance of the building served as a promenade in which visitors could take in the sweeping views. The peak is called Overlook for a reason. What's more, the advertisement stated that "the grounds are laid out with walks, croquet grounds, summer houses, etc."[142] In short, it was a playground for the wealthy, offering a plethora of entertainments and modern conveniences. As such, visits to Catskill mountain houses, such as Overlook, increasingly supplanted the once-common summer trip to Europe.

In the summer of 1873, the hotel attracted the attention of the then president Ulysses S. Grant. He stayed for two days. Upon his arrival, guests on the piazza showered him with flowers and excitedly went forth to meet the war hero turned president. During his time at the hotel, he journeyed to the summit of the mountain with a procession of at least a hundred people. "During the ascent," one newspaper article noted, "which was led by Gen. Grant and two little girls, the guests sang war choruses and patriotic songs."[143]

Two years later, on April Fool's Day 1875, the hotel caught fire and burned down. All that could be saved was a piano, silverware, and furniture from the parlor. In 1878, a newly constructed Overlook Mountain House again welcomed guests and stood until 1923, when another blaze brought the structure down. During the First World War, it was rumored that German spies used the hotel as a base to transmit secrets via radio.

After the second blaze, the decision to rebuild was made again, but this time making sure the hotel's walls were made of thick, reinforced concrete. Unfortunately, before the four-story building was completed, the owner died. His grandson was tasked with finishing it but, before doing so, decided to enlist in the armed forces right around the start of World War II. When he returned, he found the building vandalized and most items of value inside stolen. Construction of the Overlook Mountain House never resumed.

Today, the abandoned structure continues to decay, with only its fireproof concrete shell remaining. Yet another fire took down the roof and all other flammable items inside during the 1960s. Nature is slowly reclaiming the once-bustling grounds. Trees of significant size rise high within and around the building, and lush arrays of wildflowers decorate the muddy floors of several rooms.

Half a mile farther up the mountain, another relic graces the summit of Overlook. A 60-foot-high fire tower decommissioned in 1988 steadily draws visitors, who ascend the seemingly flimsy structure to take in the sweeping views. To the north and west rise the wooded Catskills, punctuated in one spot by an inland sea known as the Ashokan Reservoir. Meanwhile, a scan to the south or east reveals a thin blue ribbon snaking across the comparatively flat landscape. The mighty Hudson from this height looks little more than a minor stream.

Nervous about climbing an aging fire tower? Several popular cliffs within a two-minute walk of the tower offer comparable views.

Serpent Petroform?

Recently, prior to the construction of a radio tower on the mountain, a series of mysterious stone walls and cairns were discovered on the southeastern slope of Overlook. The fifty-four structures range in size from only a few feet in length to around 100 feet. While the vast majority are under 10 feet in length and are more or less randomly distributed throughout the forest, the larger structures (eight in total) appear to form the constellation Draco. Six linear mounds of stacked stone and two serpentine stone walls compose the petroform. The latter appear to be snake effigies and consist of undulating stone walls triangular in dimension that terminate at glacial erratics. The large boulders presumably serve as the serpents' heads. When we connect the dots, as it were, between these structures, all of which are 50 or more feet in length, a startlingly precise mirror image of the constellation Draco emerges.

One leading theory is that these structures were created by Native Americans. Some have speculated that a few of the larger cairns might be burial markers. Moreover, the snake effigies might indicate the location of underground waterways or springs. Taken as a whole, however, the Draco petroform likely has a more spiritual connotation.

To numerous ancient cultures, Draco represented a dragon or serpent. To the Algonquin tribes of the Northeast, according to the archeologist and anthropologist Edward Lenik, "Snakes were considered to be messengers to the underworld who inspired fear and respect."[144] In native religion and mythology, beings known as "horned

In 1940, the unfinished third incarnation of the Overlook Mountain House was boarded up.

Trees and other lush vegetation decorate many of the ruins' rooms.

serpents" wielded immense strength and power. Despite the serpents instilling fear and being viewed as villains in many tales, the qualities these beings possessed were often revered, and therefore the serpents themselves were worthy of worship to a degree.

As it turns out, Draco can be seen directly overhead of Overlook Mountain. In his book *Spirits in Stone*, Glenn Kreisberg states that to the "early sky watchers living in the Hudson River valley, occupying lands for miles to the south, east, and west, Overlook Mountain would have been the place to look toward to see the Serpent of the North."[145] What's more, is it mere coincidence that the mountain has one of the highest concentrations of rattlesnakes in New York State? To the native peoples, the pervasive serpent symbolism may have caused them to believe that the mountain possessed great power and therefore was considered sacred. All of this put together lends significant strength to the argument of Native American creation.

Nonetheless, most mainstream archeologists are skeptical at best of the supposed "petroforms," believing that the stacked-stone structures arose when sheep pasture was being cleared in the not-too-distant past. While nearby rockshelters toward the base of Overlook were used by Native Americans thousands of years ago, no clear evidence as of yet has definitively linked the cairns and walls to ancient Native Americans. Perhaps one day through thorough archeological excavations and the like, the mystery of these intriguing stone mounds will finally be solved.

Getting There

Parking for the Overlook Mountain Trail is located directly across the road from the KTD Tibetan Buddhist Temple (352 Meads Mountain Road, Woodstock, NY 12498). From the trailhead, follow the red-blazed carriage road up the mountain. In about 1.5 miles the ruins of the Overlook Mountain House will come into view on the right. Sections of the structure are in rough shape—exercise caution if you venture near it.

At 1.8 miles from the parking area, the first trail junction appears. It is here that one must decide whether to venture to the top of the mountain or to proceed downhill to Echo Lake.

For those looking to visit the summit and fire tower, stay to the right, continuing along the carriage road for 0.3 miles. Aside from the views offered by the fire tower, another excellent spot to take in the scenery is at a cliff called the Eagle's Nest. At the cabin, follow an unmarked footpath east for a minute until the overlook is reached. Legend has it that at this location, an eagle killed an Indian child that it had snatched up in its talons and carried away from elsewhere.

Taking a left at the trail junction leads to Echo Lake via the blue-blazed Overlook Trail. Follow it for 1.3 miles until another junction is reached. Bear left and follow the yellow-blazed Echo Lake Trail for 0.6 miles. A lean-to and numerous campsites are scattered around the lake. Fishing is allowed, but the use of baitfish is prohibited. Keep in mind that rattlesnakes and bears are prevalent in the area.

Acknowledgments

I owe several people gratitude for their invaluable assistance to help bring this book to fruition. I thank the following individuals: Michael Frazier of the Rhinebeck Historical Society for helping to clarify the boundaries of historic land tracts and tracing their ownership over the centuries. Gregory Sokaris, the executive director of the Wilderstein Historic Site, for providing permission to photograph the grounds of the estate. The individuals at Historic Huguenot Street for allowing me to photograph the grounds of one of the country's oldest streets. Patrick Raftery of the Westchester County Historical Society for providing documents relating to Raven Rock. Mike Kudish for helping direct me to information regarding Platte Clove's many waterfalls. Andrew Jaouen for his input on the King's Chamber and other stone chambers of Putnam County. And last, but not least, Meagan Clark, Christina Haering, Ted Hsu, and others who accompanied me on my ramblings to investigate and photograph the sites in this book.

Endnotes

1. The Capture of Major John André

1. William Abbatt, *The Crisis of the Revolution* (New York: William Abbatt, 1899), 29.
2. Robert Bolton, *A History of the County of Westchester*, vol. 1 (New York: Alexander S. Gould, 1848), 224.
3. Nathaniel Philbrick, *Valiant Ambition: George Washington, Benedict Arnold, and the Fate of the American Revolution* (New York: Penguin Books, 2017), 315.
4. James Thacher, *Military Journal of the American Revolution* (Hartford, CT: Hurlbut Williams, 1862), 228.
5. Edgar Mayhew Bacon, *Chronicles of Tarrytown and Sleepy Hollow*, 6th ed. (New York: Knickerbocker, 1905), 103.
6. Washington Irving, *Rip Van Winkle and The Legend of Sleepy Hollow* (New York: Macmillan, 1893), 200.
7. Ibid., 198.
8. Ibid., 190.
9. Ibid., 198.
10. Ibid., 199.
11. Benson J. Lossing, *The Two Spies, Nathan Hale and John André* (New York: D. Appleton, 1903), 75.

2. Raven Rock

12. Irving, *Rip Van Winkle and The Legend of Sleepy Hollow*, 190.
13. Bacon, *Chronicles of Tarrytown and Sleepy Hollow*, 112.
14. Bolton, *A History of the County of Westchester*, vol. 1, 349.
15. Bacon, *Chronicles of Tarrytown and Sleepy Hollow*, 113.
16. Ibid.
17. Minna Irving, "In Washington Irving's Country," *New Age Magazine*, July 1905, 20.

3. Bear Rock Petroglyph

18. Nathaniel Philbrick, *Mayflower: A Story of Courage, Community, and War* (New York: Penguin Group, 2006), 105.
19. Nicholas A. Shoumatoff, "The Bear Rock Petroglyphs Site," *The Bulletin* 55 (July 1972): 3.
20. Adriaen van der Donck, *A Description of New Netherland*, ed. Charles T. Gehring and William A. Starna, trans. Diederik Willem Goedhuys (Lincoln: University of Nebraska Press, 2008), 71.

21. Evan T. Pritchard, *Native New Yorkers: The Legacy of the Algonquin People of New York* (San Francisco: Council Oak Books, 2002), 166.
22. William M. Beauchamp, *Aboriginal Place Names of New York* (Albany: New York State Education Department, 1907), 249.

4. Croton Point

23. Tina Kelley, "In Their Footsteps," *New York Times*, May 2, 2004, WC14.
24. Robert Bolton, *The History of the Several Towns, Manors, and Patents of the County of Westchester*, vol. 1 (New York: Cadmus, 1881), 84.
25. Benson J. Lossing, *The Hudson, from the Wilderness to the Sea* (New York: Virtue and Yorston, 1866), 303.
26. Daniel Wise, *Summer Days on the Hudson* (New York: Nelson & Phillips, 1875), 103–104.
27. H. L. Barnum, *The Spy Unmasked* (New York: J&J Harper, 1828), 149.
28. New York State Legislature, *Documents of the Assembly of the State of New York*, vol. 18 (Albany, NY: J. B. Lyon, 1917), 288.
29. Charles M. Skinner, *Myths and Legends of Our Own Land*, vol. 1 (Philadelphia: J. B. Lippincott, 1896), 57.
30. Ibid., 58.
31. Charles G. Hine, *The New York and Albany Post Road* (New York: C. G. Hine, 1905), 32.
32. "Revives Tradition of Captain Kidd's Famous Buried Treasure," *Scarsdale Inquirer*, December 13, 1934, 1.
33. Wise, *Summer Days on the Hudson*, 104.

5. Bloody Pond & the Twin Forts of the Hudson Highlands

34. Benson J. Lossing, *Pictorial Field Guide of the Revolution*, vol. 1 (New York: Harper & Brothers, 1859), 731.
35. Continental Congress of the United States, *Secret Journals of the Acts and Proceedings of Congress*, vol. 1 (Boston: Thomas B. Wait, 1821), 13.
36. Lossing, *Pictorial Field Guide of the Revolution*, vol. 1., 733.
37. Ibid.
38. George A. Blauvelt, "Bear Mountain," *Quarterly Journal of the New York Historical Association* 19 (1921): 25.
39. John W. Barber and Henry Howe, *Historical Collections of the State of New York* (New York: Barber & Howe, 1842), 422.
40. Timothy Dwight, *Travels in New-England and New-York*, vol. 3 (New Haven, CT: Timothy Dwight, 1822), 435–36.
41. Ibid.
42. Ibid., 436.
43. Ernest Ingersoll, *Rand McNally & Co.'s Illustrated Guide to the Hudson River and Catskill Mountains* (Chicago: Rand, McNally, 1893), 79.
44. "The Ghosts of Lake Assinnipink," *The Publicist* 1 (1918): 23.

6. Claudius Smith Den

45. Philip H. Smith, *Legends of the Shawangunk and Its Environs* (Pawling, NY: Smith, 1887), 60.
46. Ibid.
47. Ibid., 61.
48. Ibid.
49. Ibid., 63.
50. P. Demarest Johnson, "The Ramapo Valley," ed. Marion Harland, *The Home-Maker*, April–September 1890, 394.
51. Smith, *Legends of the Shawangunk and Its Environs*, 63.
52. Ibid., 64.
53. "Deed of the Cow-Boys: Claudius Smith's Terrible Gang in Revolutionary Days," *New York Times*, November 23, 1879, 5.
54. James Eldridge Quinlan, *History of Sullivan County* (Liberty, NY: G. M. Beebe & W. T. Morgans, 1873), 470.
55. Max Schrabisch, "Horsestable Rock the Ancient Haunt of Indian and Outlaw," *Americana*, January–July 1911, 118.

7. Stone Chambers of Putnam County

56. John Pynchon, *The Pynchon Papers*, vol. 1, ed. Carl Bridenbaugh (Boston: Colonial Society of Massachusetts, 1982), 12.
57. Fred N. Brown, *Rediscovering Vinland: Evidence of Ancient Viking Presence in America* (New York: iUniverse, 2009), 128.
58. Roger Williams, *Roger Williams' Key to the Indian Language*, vol. 1 (Providence, RI: John Miller, 1827), 67.
59. Ibid., 68.

8. Hawk Rock

60. Edward J. Lenik, Thomas Fitzpatrick, and Nancy L. Gibbs, "A Twentieth-Century Petroglyph on Horse Pound Brook," *The Bulletin* 105 (Spring 1993): 3.
61. Kevin Flynn, "A Hike into the Mystic, or Just a Walk in the Woods?," *New York Times*, October 24, 2010, C25.
62. Philip J. Imbrogno, "The Mysteries of Hawk Rock," *Connecticut Post*, September 8, 2010, www.ctpost.com/default/article/The-mysteries-of-Hawk-Rock-649692.php.

9. Balanced Rock

63. John Finch, "On the Celtic Antiquities of America," *American Journal of Science and Arts* 7, no. 1 (1824): 152.
64. Ibid., 150.
65. Ibid., 153.

66. J. Piggot, "Editor's Box," ed. J. Erskine Clarke, *Stinchcombe Parish Magazine*, 1867, 110.
67. Bolton, *The History of the Several Towns, Manors, and Patents of the County of Westchester*, vol. 1, 767.
68. Ibid., 768.

10. Indian Brook Falls

69. Nathaniel Parker Willis, *American Scenery*, vol. 1 (London: George Virtue, 1840), 85.
70. Ibid., 86.
71. E. Thomson, ed., "The Indian Falls near Cold Spring," *Ladies' Repository*, August 1845, 225.
72. "Indian Falls, Cold Spring, N.Y." *Dollar Monthly Magazine*, July 1864, 439.
73. Thomson, "The Indian Falls near Cold Spring," 225.
74. Willis, *American Scenery*, vol. 1, 85.
75. *Putnam County Recorder*, 1880, quoted in Peter Lourie, *River of Mountains* (Syracuse, NY: Syracuse University Press, 1995), 302.

11. Pollepel Island

76. Jasper Dankens, "Jasper Dankers 1680," in *Chronicles of the Hudson*, 2nd ed., ed. Roland Van Zandt (Hensonville, NY: Black Dome, 1998), 34.
77. Evan T. Pritchard, *Henry Hudson and the Algonquins of New York* (San Francisco: Council Oak Books, 2009), 221.
78. Quinlan, *History of Sullivan County*, 499.
79. Washington Irving, *Dolph Heyliger*, ed. George H. Browne (Boston: D. C. Heath, 1904), 67.
80. Ibid., 68.
81. Benson J. Lossing, "Names in the Valley of the Hudson," *The Independent*, November 2, 1884, 4.
82. "Explosion Wrecks Bannerman Arsenal," *New York Times*, August 16, 1920, 10.

12. Huguenot Street (New Paltz)

83. Ralph LeFevre, *History of New Paltz, New York and Its Old Families* (Albany, NY: Fort Orange, 1903), 11.
84. Ibid.
85. Ibid., 2.
86. "Horrid Murder and Suicide," *Guardian; or, New Brunswick Advertiser*, October 8, 1801, 2.
87. Ibid.
88. Ibid.
89. Ibid.

13. Sam's Point

90. Evan T. Pritchard, *Native American Stories of the Sacred* (Woodstock, VT: Skylight Paths, 2005), 80.
91. Smith, *Legends of the Shawangunk and Its Environs*, 133.
92. Pritchard, *Native New Yorkers: The Legacy of the Algonquin People of New York*, 259.
93. Quinlan, *History of Sullivan County*, 395.

14. Dover Stone Church

94. James H. Smith, *History of Dutchess County, New York* (Syracuse, NY: D. Mason, 1882), 482.
95. Philip H. Smith, *General History of Duchess County: From 1609 to 1876, Inclusive* (Pawling, NY: Philip H. Smith, 1877), 150.
96. George Burbank Shattuck, *Some Geological Rambles near Vassar College* (Poughkeepsie, NY: Vassar College Press, 1907), 12.
97. "Dover Stone Church," *Family Magazine* 3 (1843): 14.
98. Benson J. Lossing, "Dover Stone Church," *Poughkeepsie Casket*, December 15, 1838, 137.
99. Frank Hasbrouck, *The History of Dutchess County, New York* (Poughkeepsie, NY: S. A. Matthieu, 1909), 640.

15. Wilderstein Petroglyph

100. Edward J. Lenik, *Picture Rocks: American Indian Rock Art in the Northeast Woodlands* (Hanover, NH: University Press of New England, 2002), 171.
101. Edward M. Smith, *Documentary History of Rhinebeck, in Dutchess County, N.Y.* (Rhinebeck, NY: Edward Smith, 1881), 12.
102. Ibid., 14.
103. Ibid., 7.
104. E. M. Ruttenber, *History of the Indian Tribes of Hudson's River* (Albany, NY: J. Munsell, 1872), 15.

16. Bash Bish Falls

105. Clark W. Bryan, *The Book of Berkshire* (Great Barrington, MA: Clark W. Bryan, 1887), 150.
106. George H. Daniels, *Health and Pleasure on "America's Greatest Railroad"* (New York: New York Central & Hudson River Railroad, 1895), 106.
107. Darius Mead, ed., "Bash-Bish," *Christian Parlor Magazine*, 1854, 299.
108. Ibid., 299–300.
109. Ibid., 300.
110. Stewart H. Burnham, "A Supplementary List of Plants of Copake Falls, NY," *Torreya* 13, no. 9 (September 1913): 218.

111. S. D. Faulkner, ed., "Bash Bish," *Yale Literary Magazine*, November 1858, 63–64.
112. Mead, "Bash-Bish," 299.
113. Bryan, *The Book of Berkshire*, 153.
114. Ibid., 152.
115. *Appleton's Hand-Book of American Travel: Northern and Eastern Tour* (New York: D. Appleton, 1870), 153.
116. Henry D. Thoreau, *A Yankee in Canada* (Boston: Ticknor and Fields, 1866), 54.
117. Sereno Stetson, "The Flora of Copake Falls, N.Y.," *Torreya* 13, no. 6 (June 1913): 122.
118. Daniels, *Health and Pleasure on "America's Greatest Railroad,"* 107.

17. Spook Rock

119. Elizabeth Louise Gebhard, *The Parsonage between Two Manors*, 2nd ed. (Hudson, NY: Bryan, 1910), 217.
120. Ibid., 218.
121. Ingersoll, *Rand McNally & Co.'s Illustrated Guide to the Hudson River and Catskill Mountains*, 196.

18. Devil in the Catskills

122. Charles Lanman, *Letters from a Landscape Painter* (Boston: James Munroe, 1845), 49–50.
123. "Transcript of Death Bed Statements Made by Schultz," *New York Times*, October 26, 1935, 6.
124. Maximilian Josef Rudwin, *Devil Stories: An Anthology* (New York: Alfred A. Knopf, 1921), 289.

19. Kaaterskill Falls

125. Lossing, *The Hudson, from the Wilderness to the Sea*, 163.
126. Charles E. Hammett, "An Ideal Vacation Tour," *Outing*, April–September 1893, 149.
127. Thomas Cole, "The Falls of Kaaterskill in Winter," in *The Scenery of the Catskill Mountains*, by Washington Irving et al. (Catskill, NY: Recorder Steam Printing House, 1876), 37.
128. Ibid., 38.
129. Willis Gaylord Clark, "The 'Ollapodiana' Papers of Willis Gaylord Clark," in *The Scenery of the Catskill Mountains*, by Washington Irving et al. (Catskill, NY: Recorder Steam Printing House, 1876), 14.
130. "Where Rip Van Winkle Slept," *New York Times*, June 30, 1889, 12.
131. "A Long Mountain Drive," *New York Times*, August 20, 1882, 5.
132. Thomas Morris Longstreth, *The Catskills* (New York: Century, 1918), 95.
133. Anne Eliza Pidgeon Searing, *The Land of Rip Van Winkle* (New York: G. P. Putnam's Sons, 1884), 56.
134. Ibid., 60.
135. "A Faithful Dog's Epitaph," *New York Times*, September 1, 1901, SM5.

20. Echo Lake & Overlook Mountain

136. Irving, *Rip Van Winkle and The Legend of Sleepy Hollow*, 19–20.
137. "Summer Resorts," *New York Times*, July 19, 1874, 3.
138. Lanman, *Letters from a Landscape Painter*, 14.
139. James Pierce, "A Memoir on the Catskill Mountains," *American Journal of Science and Arts* 8 (1823): 93.
140. Searing, *The Land of Rip Van Winkle*, 98.
141. Ibid.
142. "The Overlook House," *The Sun* (New York), December 29, 1870, 3.
143. "President Grant: His Visit to Overlook Mountain," *New York Times*, July 31, 1873, 1.
144. Edward J. Lenik, "Mythic Creatures: Serpents, Dragons, and Sea Monsters in Northeastern Rock Art," *Archaeology of Eastern North America* 38 (2010): 18.
145. Glenn Kreisberg, *Spirits in Stone: The Secrets of Megalithic America* (Rochester, VT: Bear, 2018), 49.

Bibliography

"A Faithful Dog's Epitaph." *New York Times*, September 1, 1901.

"A Long Mountain Drive." *New York Times*, August 20, 1882.

Abbatt, William. *The Crisis of the Revolution*. New York: William Abbatt, 1899.

Appleton's Hand-Book of American Travel: Northern and Eastern Tour. New York: D. Appleton, 1870.

Bacon, Edgar Mayhew. *Chronicles of Tarrytown and Sleepy Hollow*. 6th ed. New York: Knickerbocker, 1905.

Barber, John W., and Henry Howe. *Historical Collections of the State of New York*. New York: Barber & Howe, 1842.

Barnum, H. L. *The Spy Unmasked*. New York: J&J Harper, 1828.

Beauchamp, William M. *Aboriginal Place Names of New York*. Albany: New York State Education Department, 1907.

Blauvelt, George A. "Bear Mountain." *Quarterly Journal of the New York Historical Association* 19 (1921): 20–32.

Bolton, Robert. *A History of the County of Westchester*. Vol. 1. New York: Alexander S. Gould, 1848.

Bolton, Robert. *The History of the Several Towns, Manors, and Patents of the County of Westchester*. Vol. 1. New York: Cadmus, 1881.

Brown, Fred N. *Rediscovering Vinland: Evidence of Ancient Viking Presence in America*. New York: iUniverse, 2009.

Bryan, Clark W. *The Book of Berkshire*. Great Barrington, MA: Clark W. Bryan, 1887.

Burnham, Stewart H. "A Supplementary List of Plants of Copake Falls, NY." *Torreya* 13, no. 9 (September 1913): 217–19.

Clark, Willis Gaylord. "The 'Ollapodiana' Papers of Willis Gaylord Clark." In *The Scenery of the Catskill Mountains*. By Washington Irving, James Fenimore Cooper, William Cullen Bryant, et al., 12–16. Catskill, NY: Recorder Steam Printing House, 1876.

Cole, Thomas. "The Falls of Kaaterskill in Winter." In *The Scenery of the Catskill Mountains*. By Washington Irving, James Fenimore Cooper, William Cullen Bryant, et al., 36–38. Catskill, NY: Recorder Steam Printing House, 1876.

Continental Congress of the United States. *Secret Journals of the Acts and Proceedings of Congress*. Vol. 1. Boston: Thomas B. Wait, 1821.

Daniels, George H. *Health and Pleasure on "America's Greatest Railroad."* New York: New York Central & Hudson River Railroad, 1895.

Dankers, Jasper. "Jasper Dankers 1680." In *Chronicles of the Hudson*. 2nd ed. Edited by Roland Van Zandt, 20–35. Hensonville, NY: Black Dome, 1998.

"Deed of the Cow-Boys: Claudius Smith's Terrible Gang in Revolutionary Days." *New York Times*, November 23, 1879.

"Dover Stone Church." *Family Magazine* 3 (1843): 14–15.

Dwight, Timothy. *Travels in New-England and New-York*. Vol. 3. New Haven, CT: Timothy Dwight, 1822.

"Explosion Wrecks Bannerman Arsenal." *New York Times*, August 16, 1920.

Faulkner, S. D., ed. "Bash Bish." *Yale Literary Magazine*, November 1858, 62–66.

Finch, John. "On the Celtic Antiquities of America." *American Journal of Science and Arts* 7, no. 1 (1824): 149–61.

Flynn, Kevin. "A Hike into the Mystic, or Just a Walk in the Woods?" *New York Times*, October 24, 2010.

Gebhard, Elizabeth Louise. *The Parsonage between Two Manors*. 2nd ed. Hudson, NY: Bryan, 1910.

"The Ghosts of Lake Assinnipink." *The Publicist* 1 (1918): 21–25.

Hammett, Charles E. "An Ideal Vacation Tour." *Outing*, April–September 1893, 148–50.

Hasbrouck, Frank. *The History of Dutchess County, New York*. Poughkeepsie, NY: S. A. Matthieu, 1909.

Hine, Charles G. *The New York and Albany Post Road*. New York: C. G. Hine, 1905.

"Horrid Murder and Suicide." *Guardian; or, New Brunswick Advertiser,* October 8, 1801.

Imbrogno, Philip J. "The Mysteries of Hawk Rock." *Connecticut Post*, September 8, 2010. www.ctpost.com/default/article/The-mysteries-of-Hawk-Rock-649692.php.

"Indian Falls, Cold Spring, N.Y." *Dollar Monthly Magazine*, July 1864, 439.

Ingersoll, Ernest. *Rand McNally & Co.'s Illustrated Guide to the Hudson River and Catskill Mountains*. Chicago: Rand, McNally, 1893.

Irving, Minna. "In Washington Irving's Country." *New Age Magazine*, July 1905, 13–20.

Irving, Washington. *Dolph Heyliger*. Edited by George H. Browne. Boston: D.C. Heath, 1904.

Irving, Washington. *Rip Van Winkle and The Legend of Sleepy Hollow*. New York: Macmillan, 1893.

Johnson, P. Demarest. "The Ramapo Valley." Edited by Marion Harland. *The Home-Maker*, April–September 1890, 385–95.

Kelley, Tina. "In Their Footsteps." *New York Times*, May 2, 2004.

Kreisberg, Glenn. *Spirits in Stone: The Secrets of Megalithic America*. Rochester, VT: Bear, 2018.

Lanman, Charles. *Letters from a Landscape Painter*. Boston: James Munroe, 1845.

LeFevre, Ralph. *History of New Paltz, New York and Its Old Families*. Albany, NY: Fort Orange, 1903.

Lenik, Edward J. "Mythic Creatures: Serpents, Dragons, and Sea Monsters in Northeastern Rock Art." *Archaeology of Eastern North America* 38 (2010): 17–37.

Lenik, Edward J. *Picture Rocks: American Indian Rock Art in the Northeast Woodlands*. Hanover, NH: University Press of New England, 2002.

Lenik, Edward J., Thomas Fitzpatrick, and Nancy L. Gibbs. "A Twentieth-Century Petroglyph on Horse Pound Brook." *The Bulletin* 105 (Spring 1993): 3–5.

Longstreth, Thomas Morris. *The Catskills*. New York: Century, 1918.

Lossing, Benson J. "Dover Stone Church." *Poughkeepsie Casket*, December 15, 1838, 137–38.

Lossing, Benson J. *The Hudson, from the Wilderness to the Sea*. New York: Virtue and Yorston, 1866.

Lossing, Benson J. "Names in the Valley of the Hudson." *The Independent*, November 2, 1884, 3–4.

Lossing, Benson J. *Pictorial Field Guide of the Revolution*. Vol. 1. New York: Harper & Brothers, 1859.

Lossing, Benson J. *The Two Spies, Nathan Hale and John André*. New York: D. Appleton, 1903.

Lourie, Peter. Quoted from *Putnam County Recorder*, 1880. In *River of Mountains*. Syracuse, NY: Syracuse University Press, 1995.

Mead, Darius, ed. "Bash-Bish." *Christian Parlor Magazine*, 1854, 298–300.

New York State Legislature. *Documents of the Assembly of the State of New York*. Vol. 18. Albany, NY: J. B. Lyon, 1917.

"The Overlook House." *The Sun* (New York), December 29, 1870.

Philbrick, Nathaniel. *Mayflower: A Story of Courage, Community, and War*. New York: Penguin Group, 2006.

Philbrick, Nathaniel. *Valiant Ambition: George Washington, Benedict Arnold, and the Fate of the American Revolution*. New York: Penguin Books, 2017.

Pierce, James. "A Memoir on the Catskill Mountains." *American Journal of Science and Arts* 8 (1823): 86–97.

Piggot, J. "Editor's Box." Edited by J. Erskine Clarke. *Stinchcombe Parish Magazine*, 1867.

"President Grant: His Visit to Overlook Mountain." *New York Times*, July 31, 1873.

Pritchard, Evan T. *Henry Hudson and the Algonquins of New York*. San Francisco: Council Oak Books, 2009.

Pritchard, Evan T. *Native American Stories of the Sacred*. Woodstock, VT: Skylight Paths, 2005.

Pritchard, Evan T. *Native New Yorkers: The Legacy of the Algonquin People of New York*. San Francisco: Council Oak Books, 2002.

Pynchon, John. *The Pynchon Papers*. Vol. 1. Edited by Carl Bridenbaugh. Boston: Colonial Society of Massachusetts, 1982.

Quinlan, James Eldridge. *History of Sullivan County*. Liberty, NY: G. M. Beebe & W. T. Morgans, 1873.

"Revives Tradition of Captain Kidd's Famous Buried Treasure." *Scarsdale Inquirer*, December 13, 1934.

Rudwin, Maximilian Josef. *Devil Stories: An Anthology*. New York: Alfred A. Knopf, 1921.

Ruttenber, E. M. *History of the Indian Tribes of Hudson's River*. Albany, NY: J. Munsell, 1872.

Schrabisch, Max. "Horsestable Rock the Ancient Haunt of Indian and Outlaw." *Americana*, January–July 1911, 112–20.

Searing, Anne Eliza Pidgeon. *The Land of Rip Van Winkle*. New York: G. P. Putnam's Sons, 1884.

Shattuck, George Burbank. *Some Geological Rambles near Vassar College*. Poughkeepsie, NY: Vassar College Press, 1907.

Shoumatoff, Nicholas A. "The Bear Rock Petroglyphs Site." *The Bulletin* 55 (July 1972): 1–5.

Skinner, Charles M. *Myths and Legends of Our Own Land*. Vol. 1. Philadelphia: J. B. Lippincott, 1896.

Smith, Edward M. *Documentary History of Rhinebeck, in Dutchess County, N.Y.* Rhinebeck, NY: Edward Smith, 1881.

Smith, James H. *History of Dutchess County, New York.* Syracuse, NY: D. Mason, 1882.

Smith, Philip H. *General History of Duchess County: From 1609 to 1876, Inclusive.* Pawling, NY: Philip H. Smith, 1877.

Smith, Philip H. *Legends of the Shawangunk and Its Environs.* Pawling, NY: Smith, 1887.

Stetson, Sereno. "The Flora of Copake Falls, N.Y." *Torreya* 13, no. 6 (June 1913): 121–37.

"Summer Resorts." *New York Times*, July 19, 1874.

Thacher, James. *Military Journal of the American Revolution.* Hartford, CT: Hurlbut, Williams, 1862.

Thomson, E., ed. "The Indian Falls near Cold Spring." *Ladies' Repository*, August 1845, 225.

Thoreau, Henry D. *A Yankee in Canada.* Boston: Ticknor and Fields, 1866.

"Transcript of Death Bed Statements Made by Schultz." *New York Times*, October 26, 1935.

van der Donck, Adriaen. *A Description of New Netherland.* Edited by Charles T. Gehring and William A. Starna. Translated by Diederik Willem Goedhuys. Lincoln: University of Nebraska Press, 2008.

"Where Rip Van Winkle Slept." *New York Times*, June 30, 1889.

Williams, Roger. *Roger Williams' Key to the Indian Language.* Vol. 1. Providence, RI: John Miller, 1827.

Willis, Nathaniel Parker. *American Scenery.* Vol. 1. London: George Virtue, 1840.

Wise, Daniel. *Summer Days on the Hudson.* New York: Nelson & Phillips, 1875.